To/ Barbara.

Every Best Wishes for 1981. The last book dealt with the Australian coastal areas, this one reflects the "Out-back".

Love
Peggy.
1981.

A SUNBURNT COUNTRY

A SUNBURNT COUNTRY

Paintings by Bill Beavan
Poetry of Dorothea Mackellar
Introductory text by Helen Bogdan

RIGBY

Rigby Limited • Adelaide • Sydney
Melbourne • Brisbane • Perth
First published 1978
In association with Creative Educational Press Pty. Ltd., Sydney

Second Edition 1979

Printed in Hong Kong

National Library of Australia
Cataloguing-in-Publication entry

BEAVAN, BILL
A SUNBURNT COUNTRY

ISBN 0 7270 0958 3
1. BEAVAN, BILL
2. PAINTINGS, AUSTRALIAN
3. AUSTRALIAN ART
I. TITLE
759.994

The type used in this book is Palatino, designed by Hermann Zapf. It was given its name in homage of one of the outstanding calligraphers of 17th century Italy, Giambattista Palatino. Filmset by The Typographers, Artarmon, N.S.W.

Contents

ACKNOWLEDGEMENTS

The publisher gratefully thanks the following for permission to reproduce copyright material in this book.

Valmai Hankel, The South Australian State Library, South Australia.
Australian Literature from its beginnings to 1935, Vol. 1. P 88 Melbourne 1940.
Landscape of Australian Poetry.

SPECIAL ACKNOWLEDGEMENT

I wish to thank my wife Helen Bogdan for the preparation of the introductory text for this book and for her encouragement and support during the course of the project.

Bill Beavan

Foreword

ONE OF THE FEW POEMS which was stamped on my memory while I was at school was Dorothea Mackellar's poem "My Country". With little prompting, I can still recite it by heart. This is probably because it vividly conjured up visions of memorable holidays I spent in the bush. The lines of the poem still stir me with a feeling of pleasant nostalgia.

The warmth and intensity of Bill Beavan's paintings affect me in much the same way. To me, therefore, the marriage of the paintings and poem in this book is a very happy one.

Before he died in 1916, the delightful artist J.J. Hilder illustrated "My Country", although with only six paintings. Hilder's soft sensitive watercolours are able to portray the more gentle aspects of our countryside—the sapphire misted mountains and the jewelled sea; but Beavan is more equipped with the style and temperament to capture that spirit of Australia which Dorothea Mackellar is trying to communicate—the flood and fire and famine, the beauty and the terror of the Australian outback.

Bill Beavan has not pursued the various art fashions that have come and gone, but has followed in the realist Australian landscape tradition, developing his individual style. He has done this most successfully, as the works illustrated in this book testify.

PAUL FITZGERALD
President,
Australian Guild of Realist Artists

Dorothea Mackellar

OVER THE YEARS since the infancy of Australian nationalism, "My Country" has become Australia's best known poem, particularly among children. It has stirred people's pride in their country and has even been suggested as a suitable national anthem. It has appeared constantly in anthologies and in the repertoires of singers and elocutionists.

Rather surprisingly, the story of the poem's author, Dorothea Mackellar, is not widely known—probably because she produced no other work which came so closely to the heart of the Australian sense of belonging. Moreover, poetry was only part of her life. She was a woman of wit and sensibility—widely travelled and a gifted linguist. Adrienne Matzenik, who nursed her for the last eleven years of her life, has drawn a pen portrait of her distinguished patient. She wrote "I was deeply impressed by her musical voice, her carriage still regal though becoming enfeebled, and the bright, alert, somewhat prominent hazel eyes which seemed to see more deeply than those of other people".

Isobel Marion Dorothea Mackellar was the only daughter of the four children of Doctor Charles Mackellar and his wife Marion. She was born at the family home at Point Piper, Sydney, on July 1, 1885.

Charles Mackellar was the son of a wealthy doctor and landowner. Born at Sydney in 1844, he studied medicine at Glasgow University and returned to establish a successful practice in Sydney. In 1903 he became a Federal Senator after forty years of service as a Member of the Legislative Council of New South Wales. His special interests lay in the field of public health, and he was recognised for his work on mental retardation and delinquency in children. He received a Knighthood in 1912 and was made a K.C.M.C. in 1916. He died in 1926.

Marion Mackellar was the sister of well known Sydney philanthropist and financier, Sir Thomas Buckland, who was born in 1848. His interests included banking, insurance, gold mining, real estate. Among his many gifts to the public was the purchase of an R.A.A.F. bomber in 1940. He died in 1947.

Dorothea Mackellar grew up in a rich and privileged home, typical of the well-to-do in the Victorian era.

The family had country properties where she spent holidays riding horses with her brothers, and her childhood memories were centred on seashore and bushland.

At the age of four she had begun to read and showed considerable intellectual capacity. She attended a private kindergarten with the State Governor's children, but was mostly educated at home by governesses. Tutors gave her extra lessons in painting and languages and she learnt fencing from an Italian who had fought under Garibaldi. She had a flair for languages and her fluency in French, Spanish, German and Italian assisted her father in their travels and in his work. She studied at Sydney University.

Doctor Charles Mackellar owned "Torreyburn", a property near Patterson, New South Wales, on the Allyn River. Wildlife abounded in those days. Dorothea loved the country even when savage droughts dried the ground until it looked like paving stones. The breaking of one drought filled her with such joy that she recalled it always. As she watched the spread of green grass across the paddocks, she kicked off her shoes and rejoiced, dancing in the rain. The incident was fresh in her mind when she wrote "My Country".

At the time of Dorothea Mackellar's adolescence, reading was one of the main relaxations of educated people. There were many publications providing possible outlets for young writers of verse and short stories. The London Spectator and Sydney Bulletin, both highly regarded journals of the day, published her work.

"My Country" was published in The Spectator in 1908.

Although Dorothea is recorded as saying that she would rather live in Australia than anywhere else, she travelled frequently overseas and knew England well.

While living in London before the First World War, she and a friend, Ruth Bedford, wrote a letter of appreciation to poet Patrick Chalmers.

He was a wealthy banker, yet a sensitive poet, and she was a romantic young woman of twenty-eight years. They fell in love and became engaged. Dorothea returned to Australia to seek her parents' approval, but war broke out and her letter to Chalmers telling of their approval was never received. The anguish of waiting in vain for word from her beloved did not stop her from writing verse, but she did not write again to Chalmers.

A strict up bringing which placed great stress upon female modesty prevented the unhappy woman from making any further advances. After five years, the war over, she made another trip to England. She found that Chalmers had married another woman in the belief that Dorothea had changed her mind.

Her feelings for Chalmers are said to be expressed in a translation from the Spanish "Dolora"—

"I forgive with all my heart
Even those I hated lately:
You, whom I have loved so greatly
Never will I pardon you!"

Her poetry began to take a deeper and more tragic tone. She continued to write during the 1920s and early 1930s and her great enthusiasm for travel was unabated until ill-health forced a more settled life.

She acquired two houses, one on the Pittwater at Lovett Bay and another called "Cintra" on Darling Point Road,

Sydney, but she spent more than ten years at Helenie Hospital, Randwick.

In the end, her great love of nature betrayed her. Against the advice of her doctors, she returned to "Cintra" and there suffered a serious fall when she got out of bed to watch birds. She was taken to the Scottish Hospital in Paddington, where she died on January 14, 1968.

Dorothea Mackellar's long life spanned a great part of Australia's history and development, but her writing reveals that her sustaining joy lay in contemplation of the beauties of the world around her. In her poem "Colour" she wrote:

"If I am tired I call on these
to help me dream."

History and Notes on the Poem

"MY COUNTRY", Dorothea Mackellar's hymn of praise to her wide, brown land, was written at a time in Australia's history when nationalism was not fashionable. The bonds of loyalty to the Motherland were strong and unquestioned.

But the young Dorothea Mackellar was fiercely proud of her colonial upbringing. She despised those who disparaged the country from which many of her friends had gained considerable wealth. The high-coloured imagery of her poem reflects the intensity of her own love for it.

An article in The Sydney Morning Herald on January 16th, 1968, claimed that Dorothea Mackellar began to write her famous poem at "Torreyburn", a property near Maitland, New South Wales. But according to Adrienne Matzenik who nursed the ailing poet towards the end of her life, the lyric was begun during an earlier visit to

England. The final draft was completed while Dorothea Mackellar was living at Buckland Chambers, Sydney, a house owned by her father.

She was constantly dissatisfied with the poem, and hesitated to submit it for publication. Three years later, when she was visiting London, it was published in "The Spectator" under the title "Core of My Heart".

The only illustrated publication of the poem appeared in 1918 in "The Art of J.J. Hilder", where it was depicted in six paintings.

The first publication in Australia seems to have been in The Sydney Morning Mail on October 21, 1908, and it later appeared in other Australian newspapers and journals. Still entitled "Core of My Heart", it was published on the Red Page of the Bulletin on April 27, 1911, in anticipation of Dorothea Mackellar's first published book of verse. On May 11, "The Closed Door and Other Verses" was reviewed on the Red Page under the heading "Opal-hearted verses". The Reviewer commented on the changed attitude of *"Australian writers of present generation"*. He wrote, *"the settled territory now appears more correctly as a warm brown land, whose droughty spasms cannot dim the radiant green and gold of her borders. Instead of being monotonous and sombre, so rich in colour is Australia that she justifies the phrase of 'an opal-hearted country' given in Dorothea Mackellar's verses printed here a fortnight ago . . . The quality of this book, its freshness and sincerity, put the author in the front rank of those who are now writing verse in Australia".*

"The Closed Door and Other Verses" marks the first use of the now familiar title of "My Country". This may account for E. Morris Miller's assumption that the poem was first published in that book.

In 1912, two anthologies—Florence Gay's "In Praise of Australia" and Bertram Stevens' "The Golden Treasury of Australian Verse"—were published. Both included "My Country" and it has since appeared in more than twenty anthologies of Australian verse. It was more popular during the twenties, but still occurs in recent anthologies for both adults and children, such as T. Inglis Moore's "From Ballads to Brennan". An inaccurate version is in Mildred Flower's "Land of Rainbow Gold".

Literary critic Brian Elliot wrote that "My Country" was written "in a mood of nostalgia or perhaps homesickness, while the poet was in Europe". But Dorothea Mackellar herself in a letter to Ian Mudie implied that she wrote in a mood of anger against *"the anti-Australianism of many Australians we knew"*. Perhaps this is the reason for the change of title from the characteristically Edwardian "Core of My Heart" to the determinedly nationalistic "My Country".

Whatever the motive for its writing, the passionate unsubtle lyric has been acclaimed by Australians for the last sixty years. In the more maturing atmosphere of Australian literature, it may not have the intellectual quality of the best modern poetry, but will always retain its sentimental appeal and its undoubted place in the history of Australia's popular literary culture.

MY COUNTRY

The love of field and coppice,
Of green and shaded lanes,
Of ordered woods and gardens
Is running in your veins;
Strong love of grey-blue distance,
Brown streams and soft, dim skies—
I know but cannot share it,
My love is otherwise.

I love a sunburnt country,
A land of sweeping plains,
Of ragged mountain ranges,
Of droughts and flooding rains.
I love her far horizons,
I love her jewel-sea,
Her beauty and her terror—
The wide brown land for me!

The stark white ring-barked forests,
All tragic to the moon,
The sapphire-misted mountains,
The hot gold hush of noon.
Green tangle of the brushes,
Where lithe lianas coil,
And orchids deck the tree-tops
And ferns the warm dark soil.

Core of my heart, my country!
Her pitiless blue sky,
When sick at heart, around us,
We see the cattle die—
But then the grey clouds gather,
And we can bless again
The drumming of an army,
The steady, soaking rain.

Core of my heart, my country!
Land of the Rainbow Gold,
For flood and fire and famine,
She pays us back threefold;
Over the thirsty paddocks,
Watch, after many days,
The filmy veil of greenness
That thickens as we gaze.

An opal-hearted country,
A wilful, lavish land—
All you who have not loved her,
You will not understand—
Though earth holds many splendours,
Wherever I may die,
I know to what brown country
My homing thoughts will fly.

I love a sunburnt country,

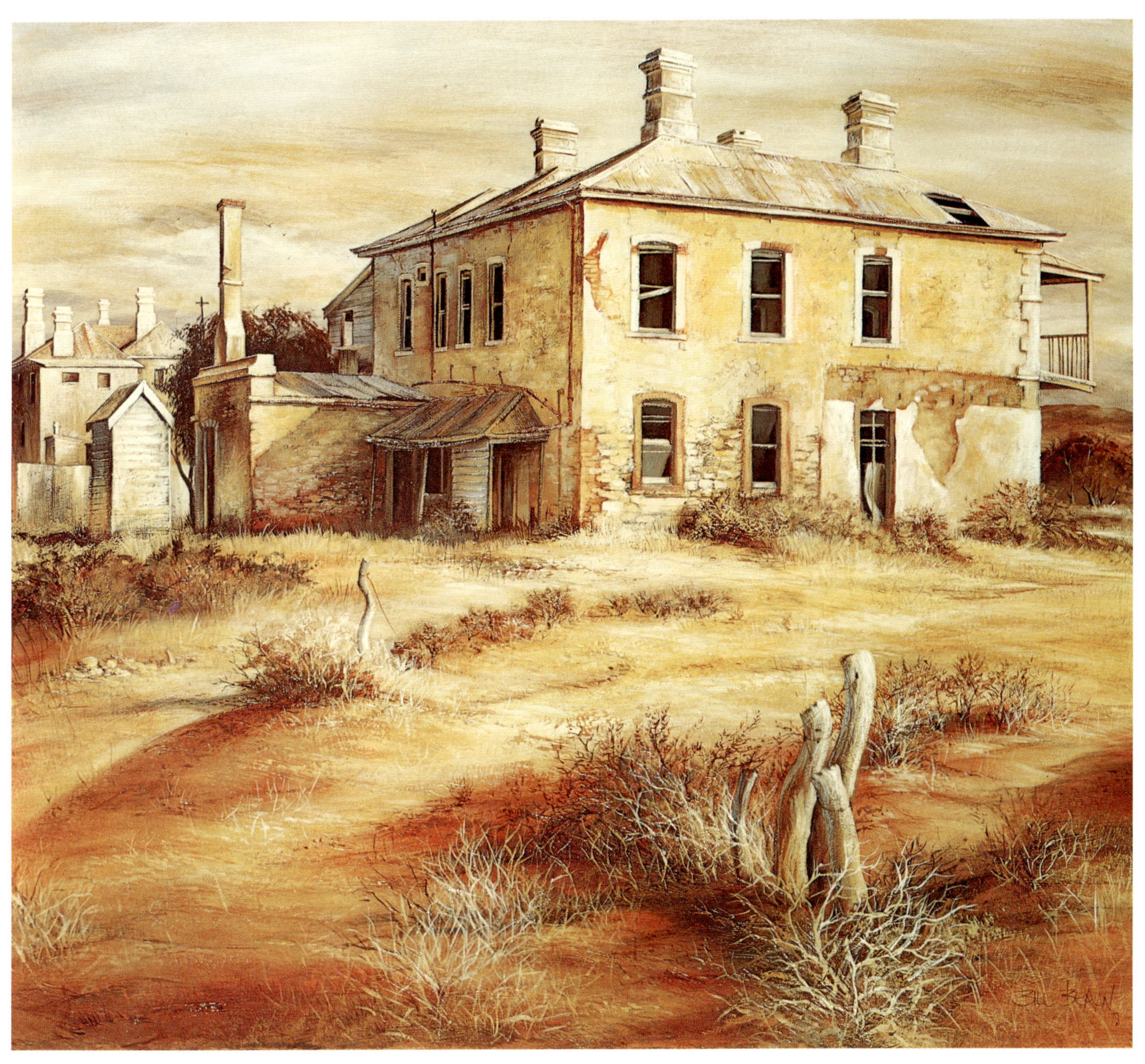

A land of sweeping plains,

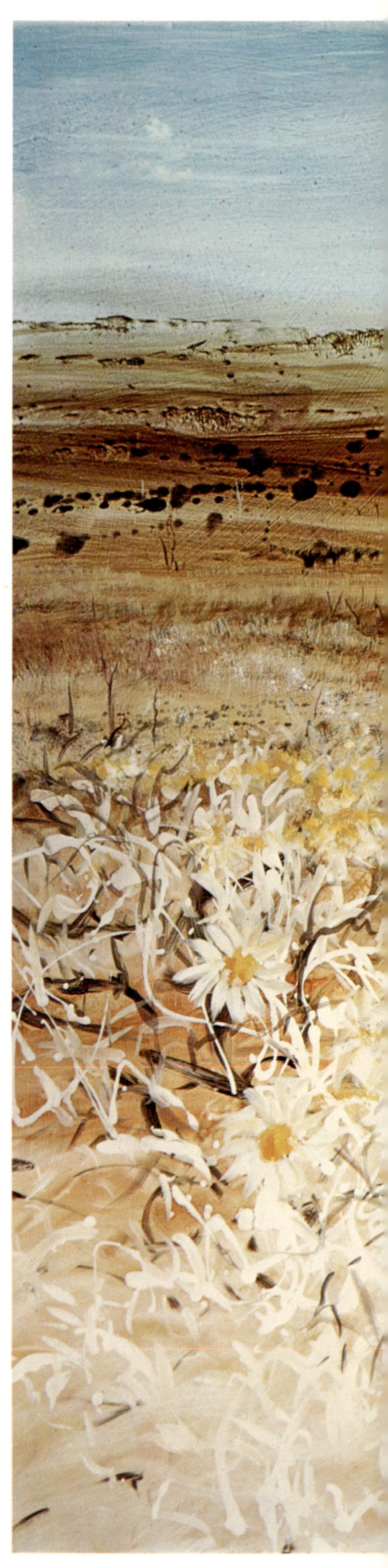

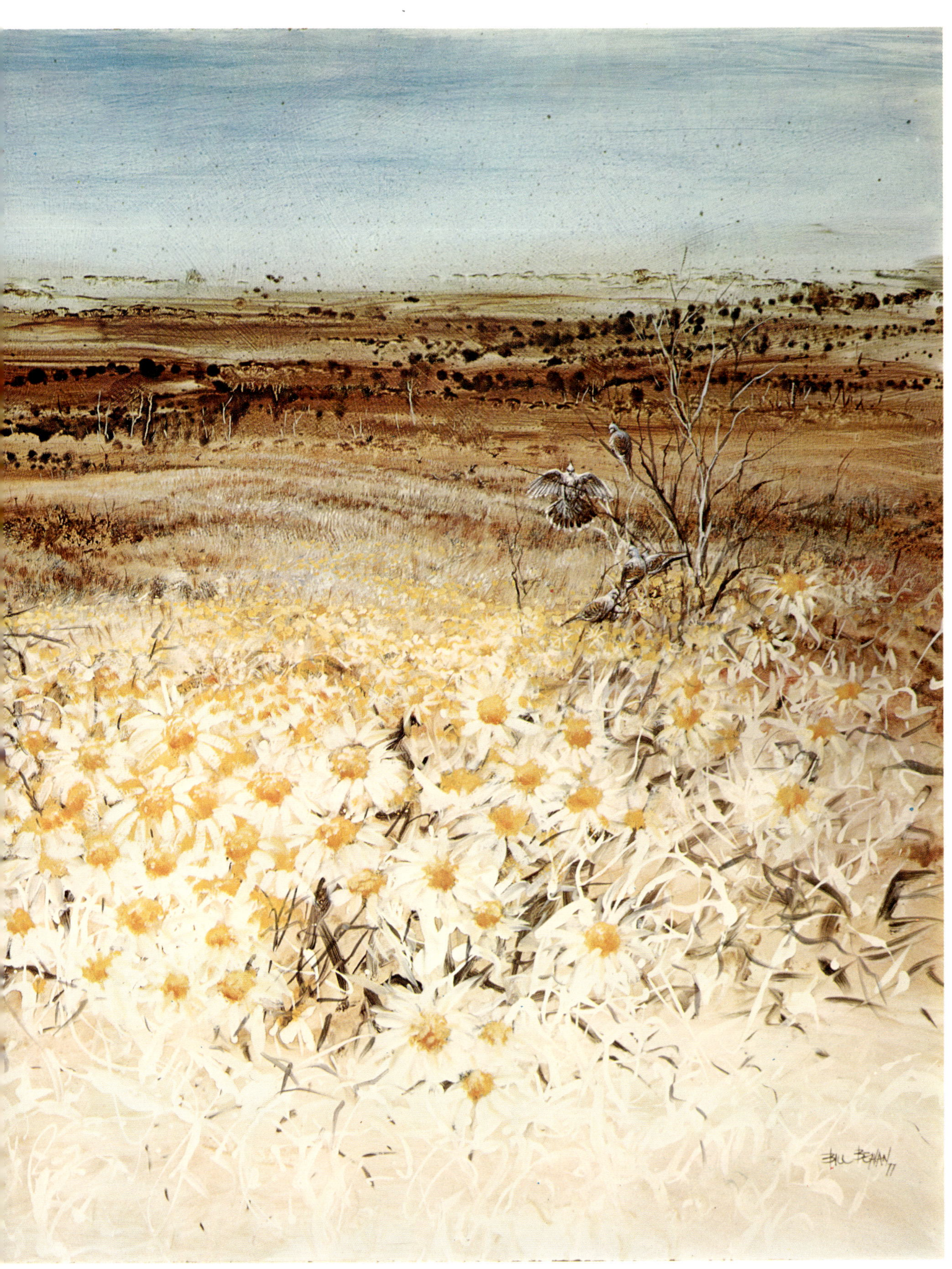

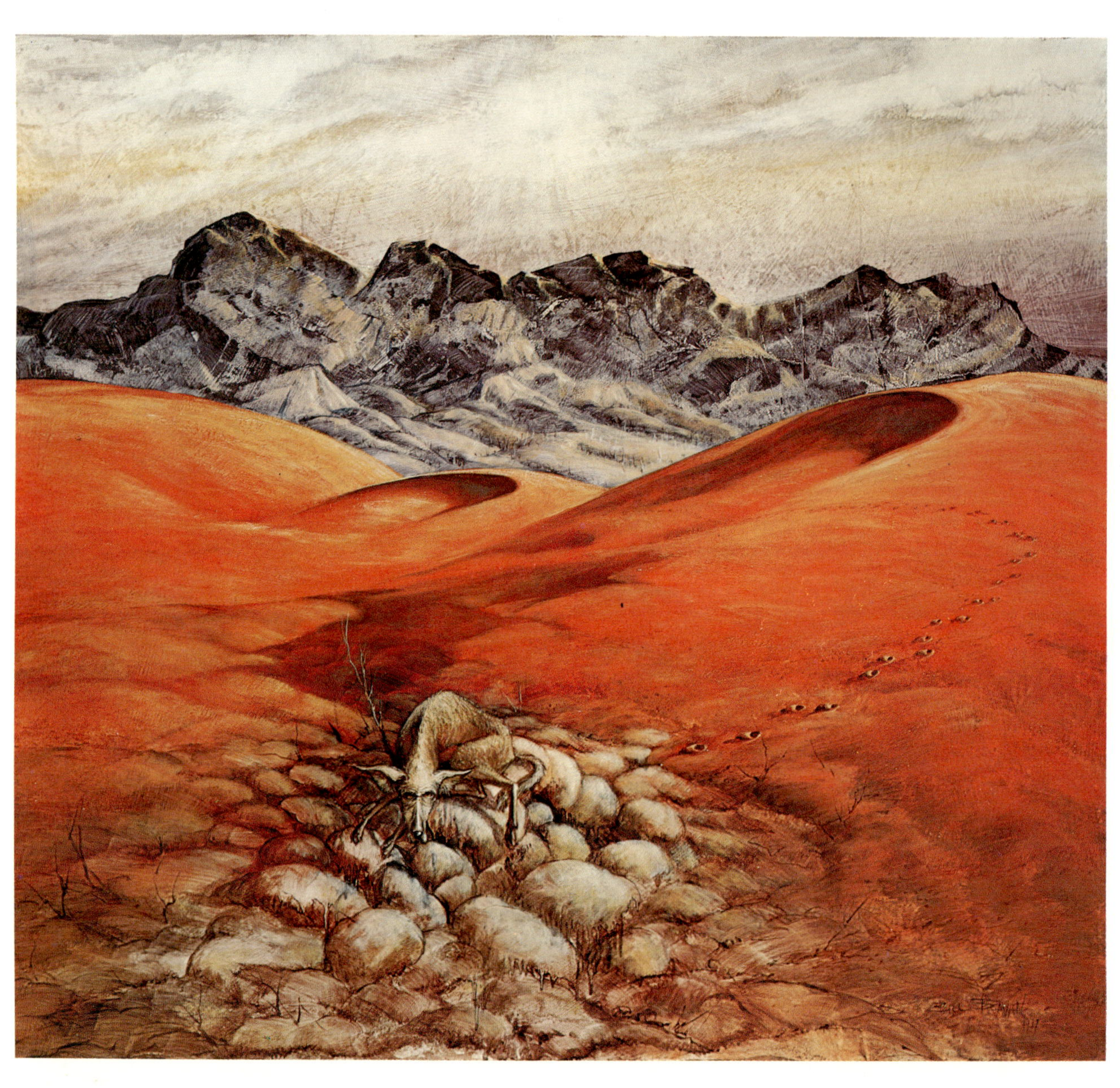

of ragged mountain ranges,

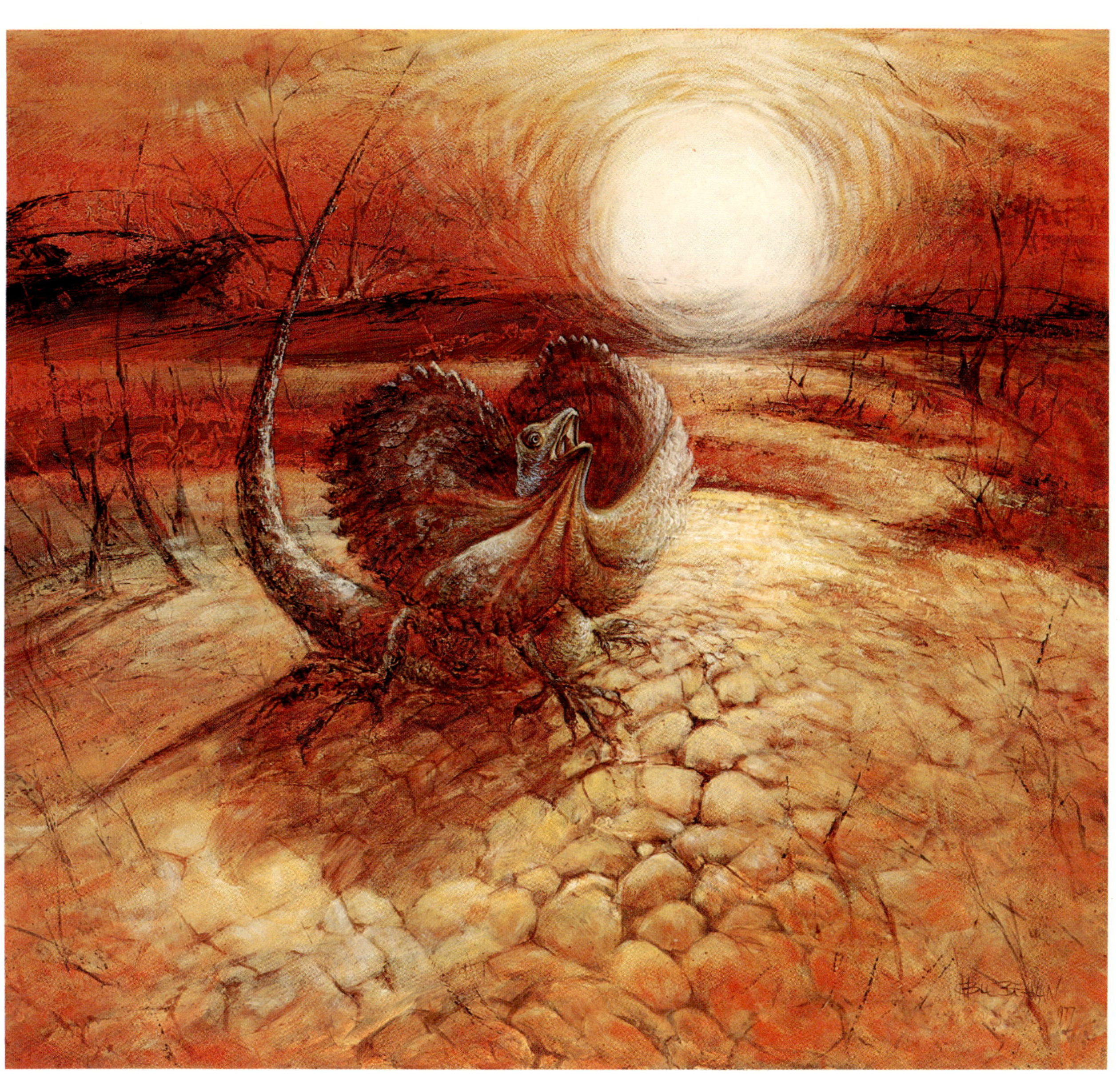

of droughts and . . .

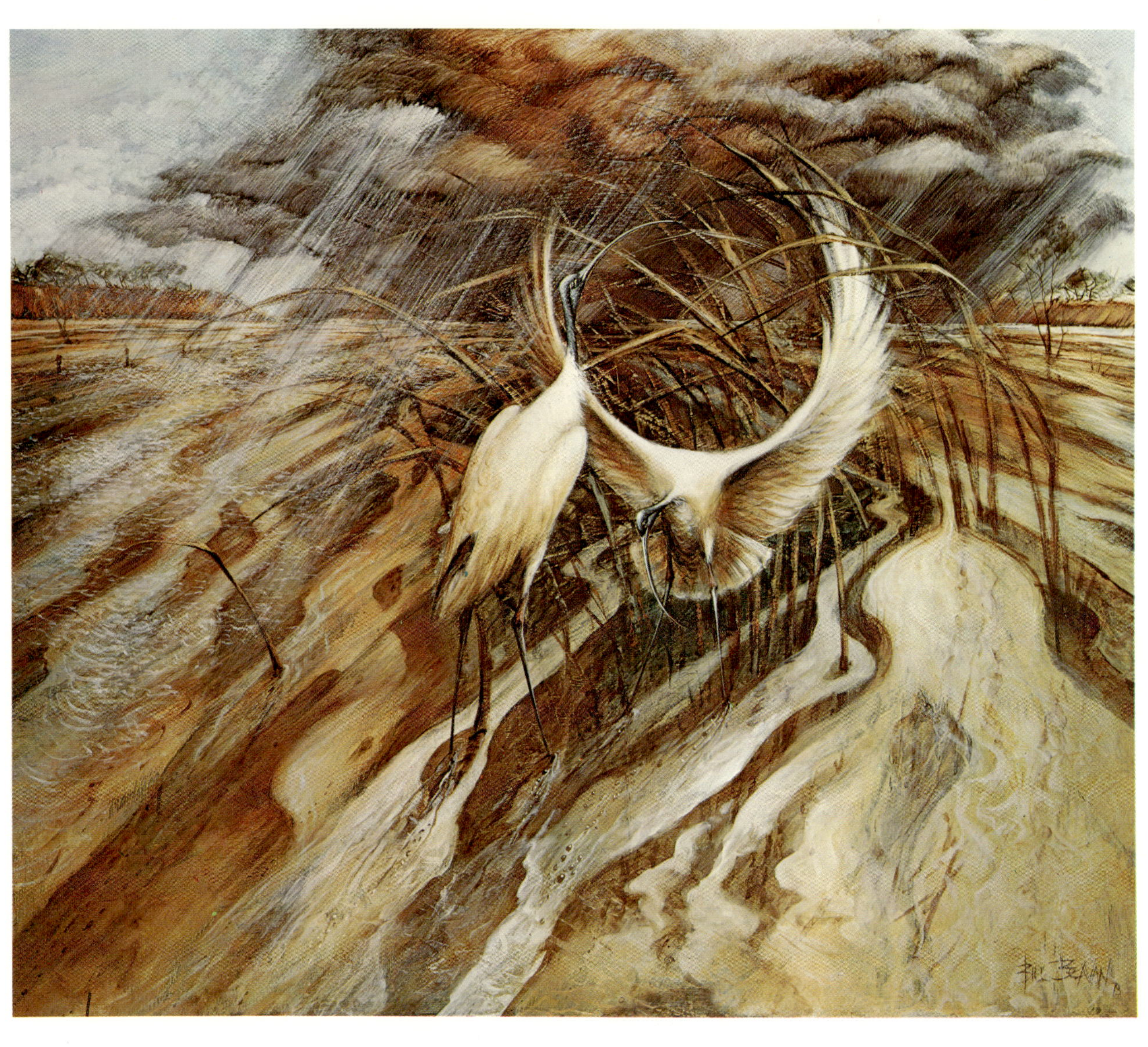

. . . flooding rains,

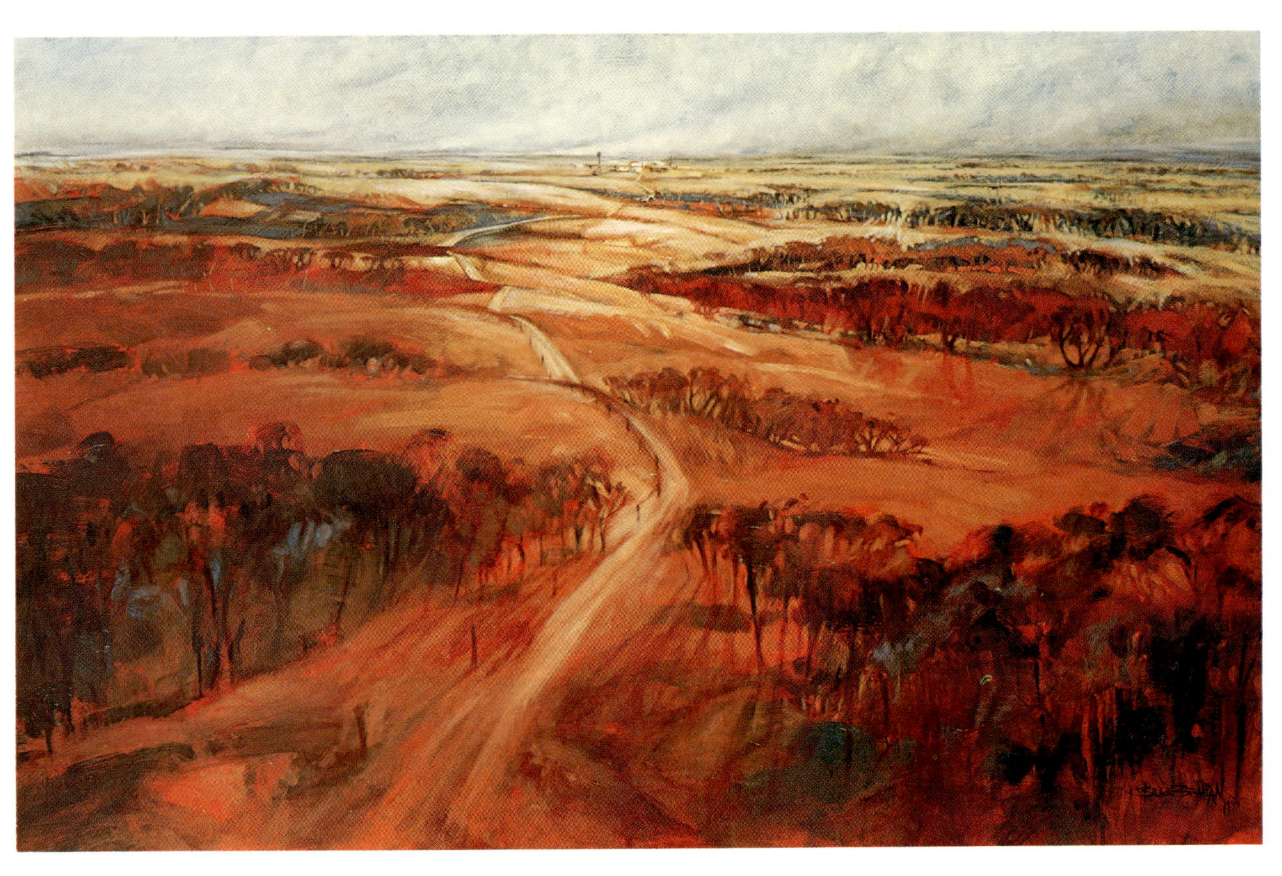

I love her far horizons,

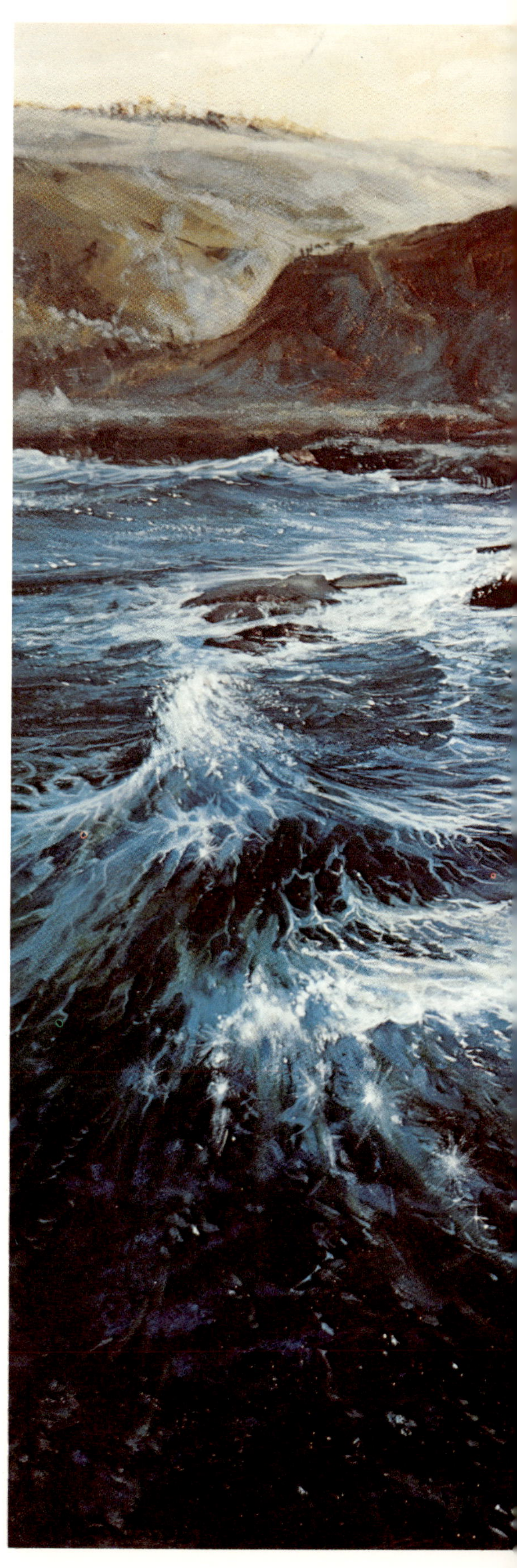

I love her jewel-sea,

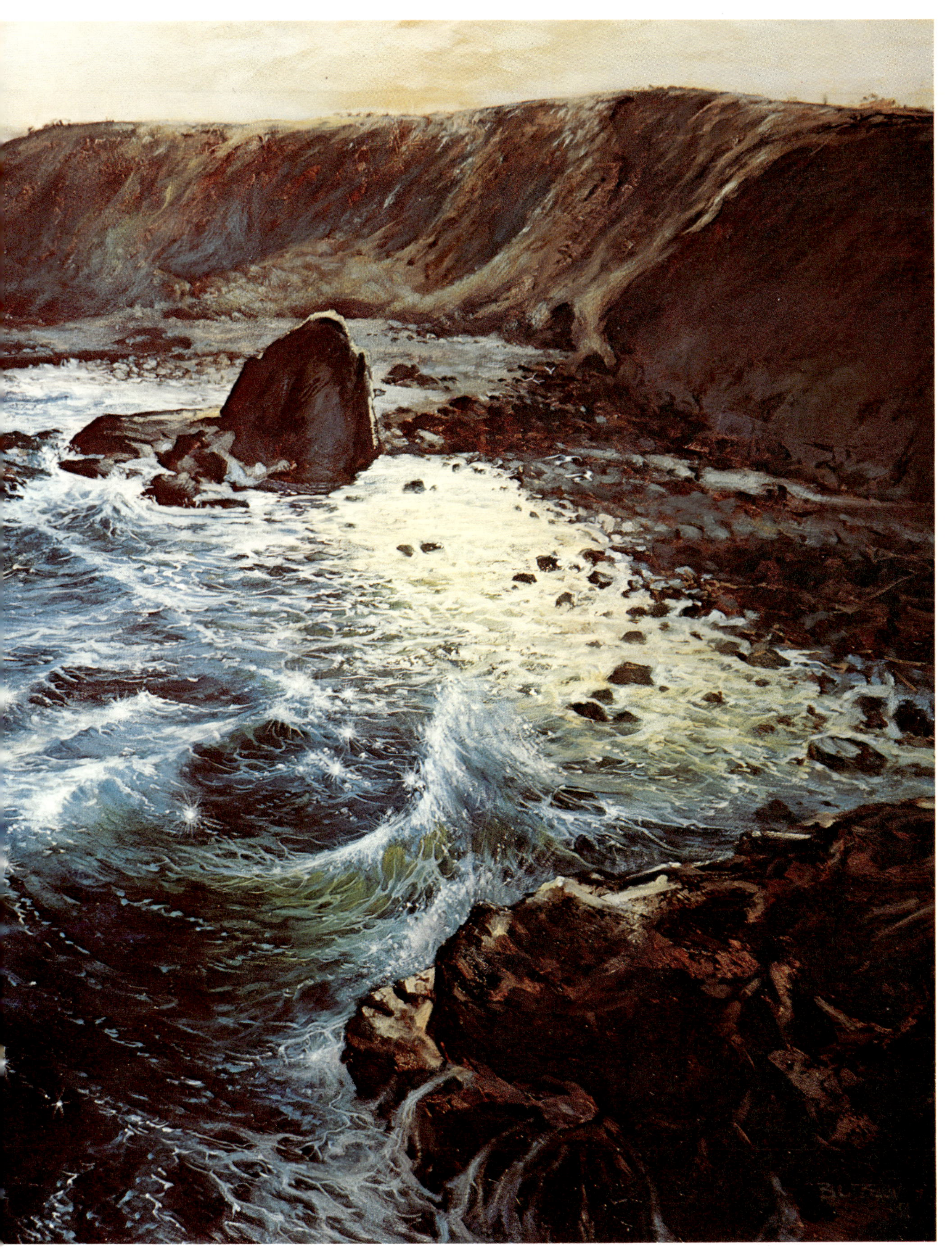

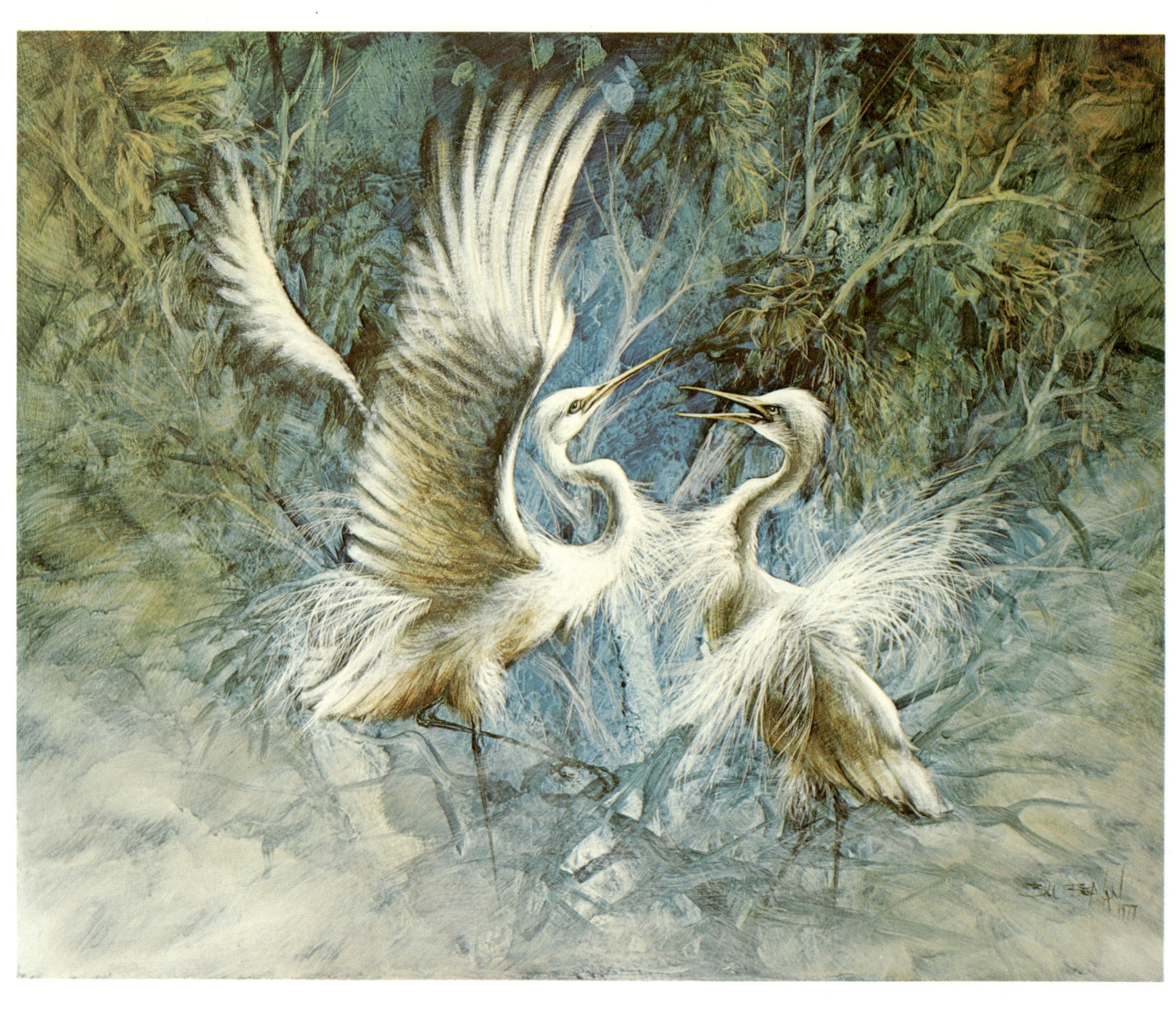

Her beauty and her terror—

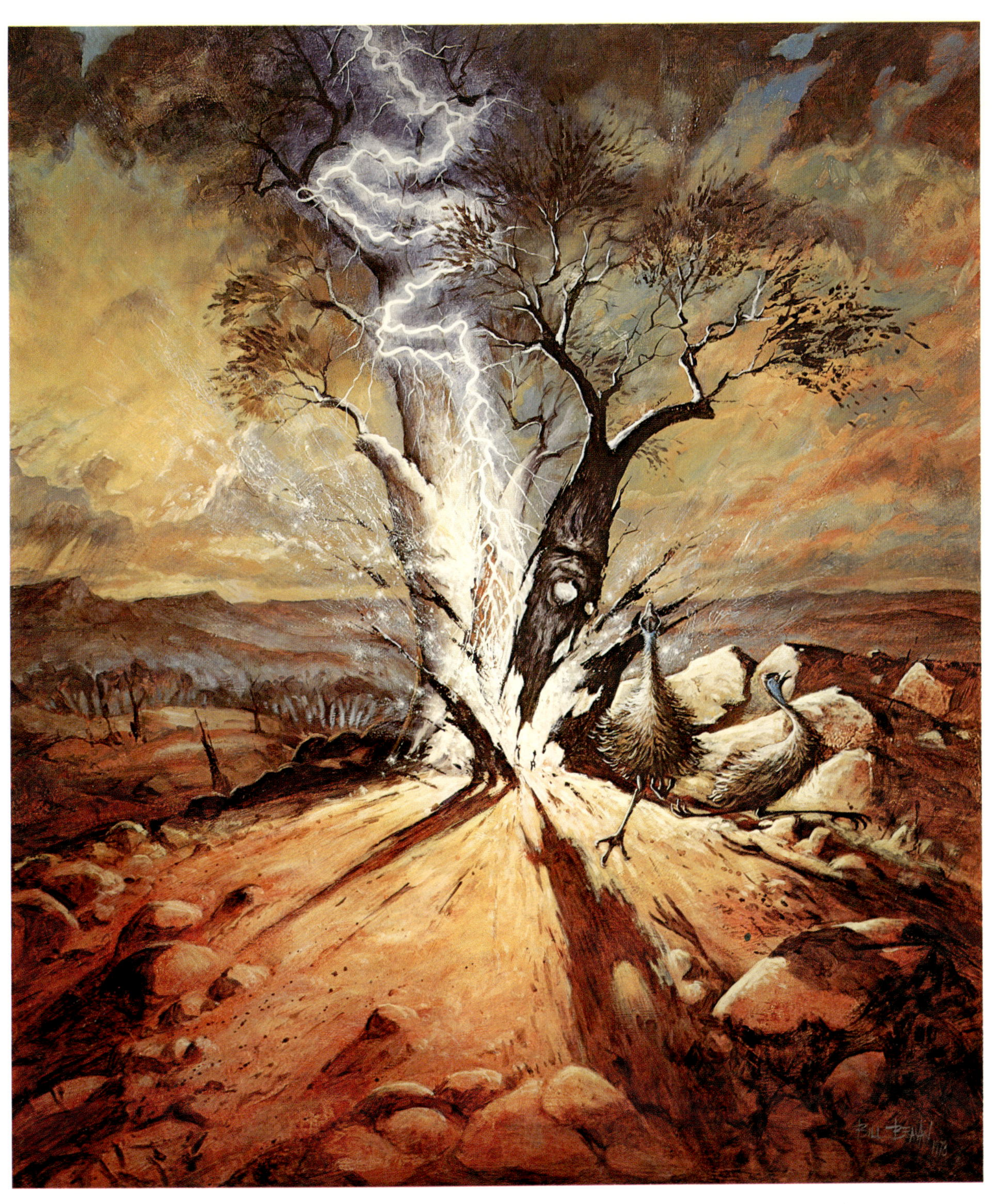

The wide brown land for me!

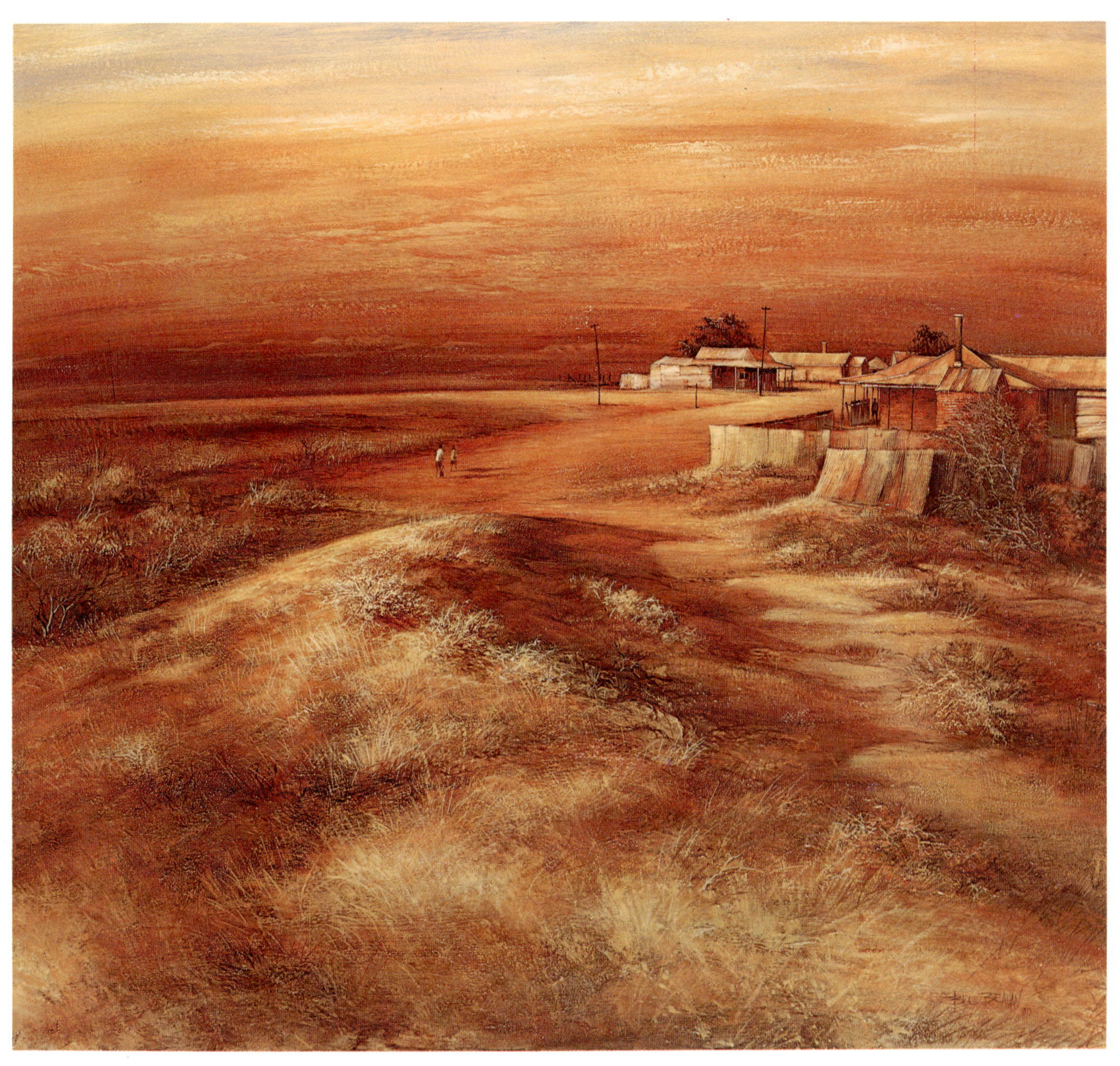

The stark white ring-barked forests,
All tragic to the moon,

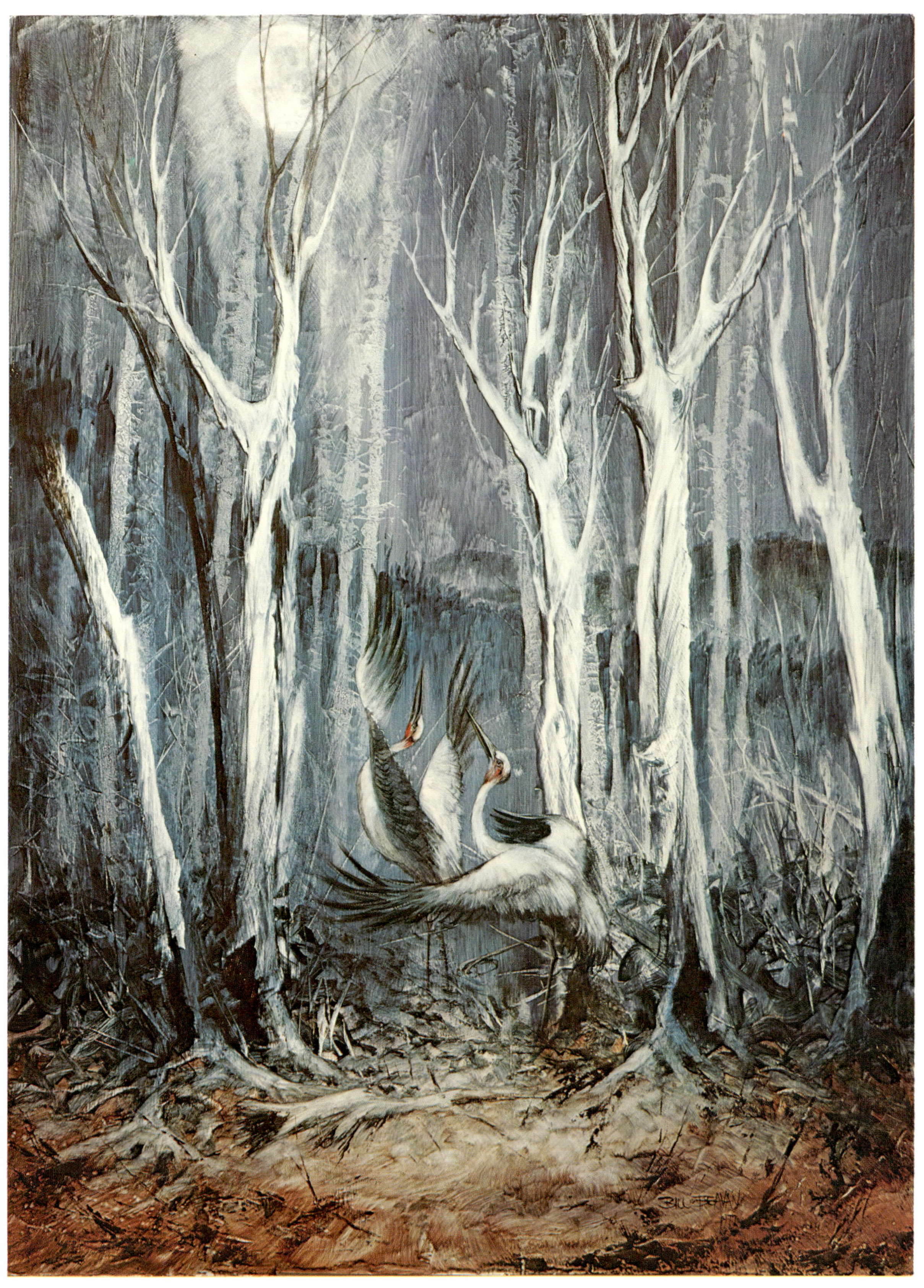

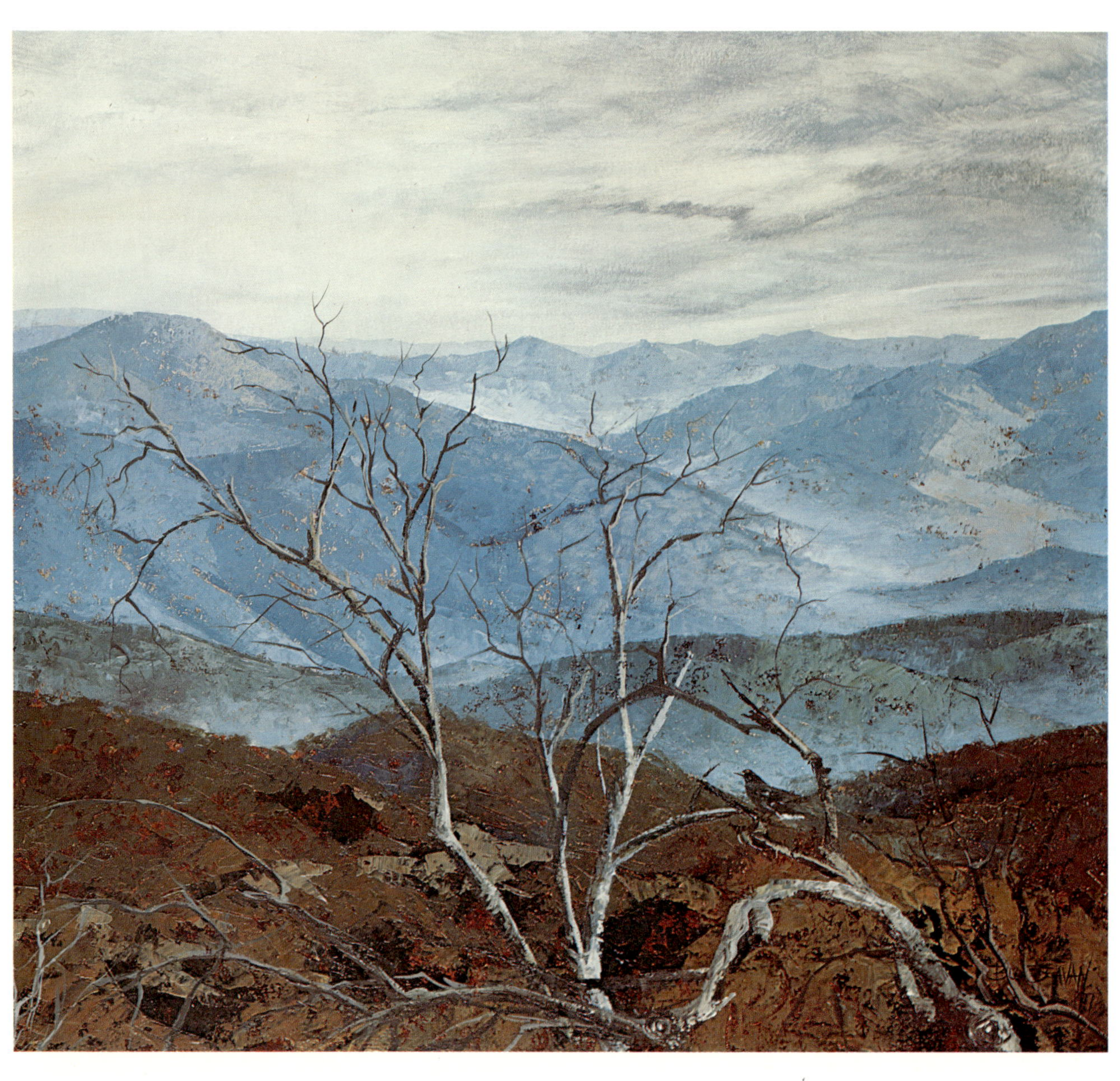

The sapphire-misted mountains,

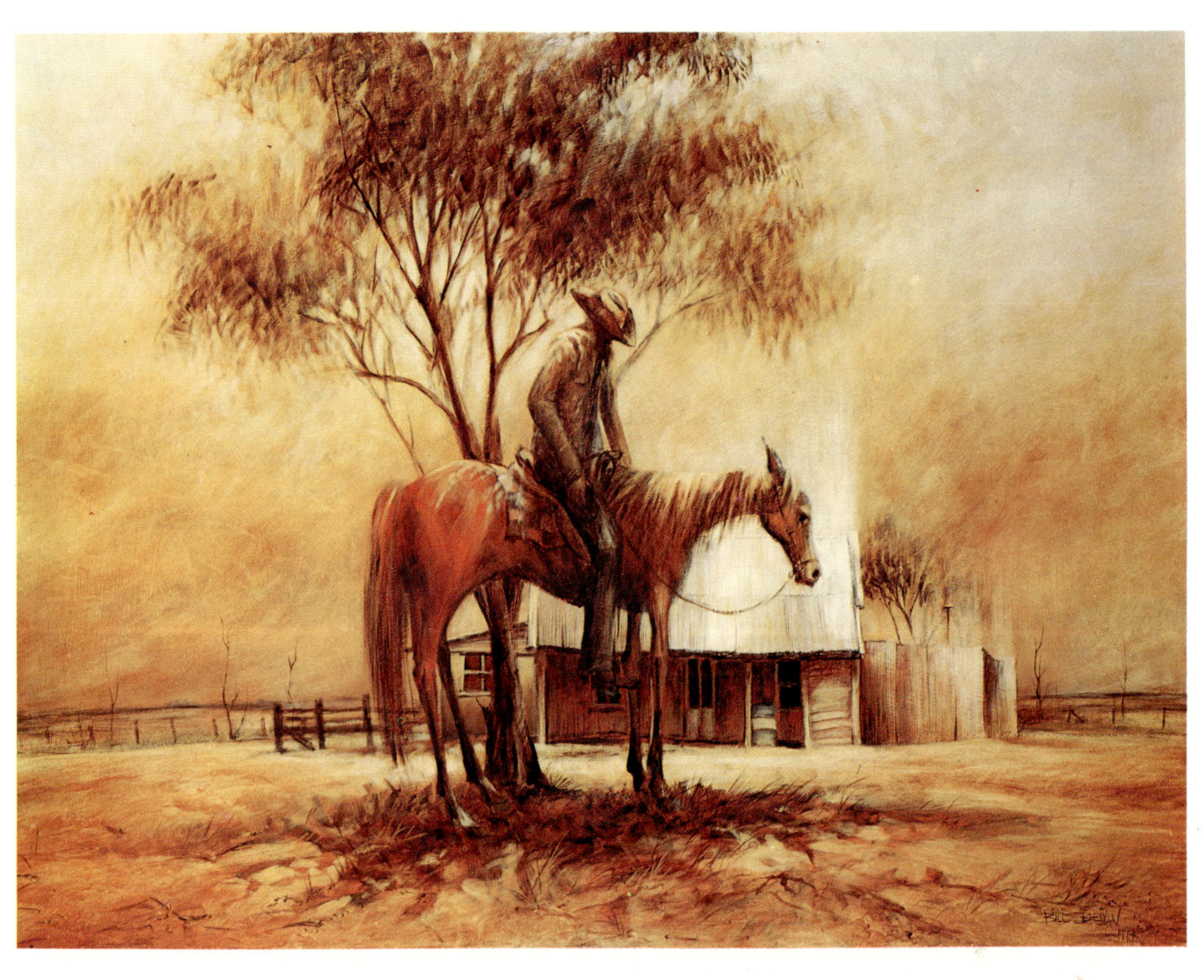

The hot gold hush of noon.

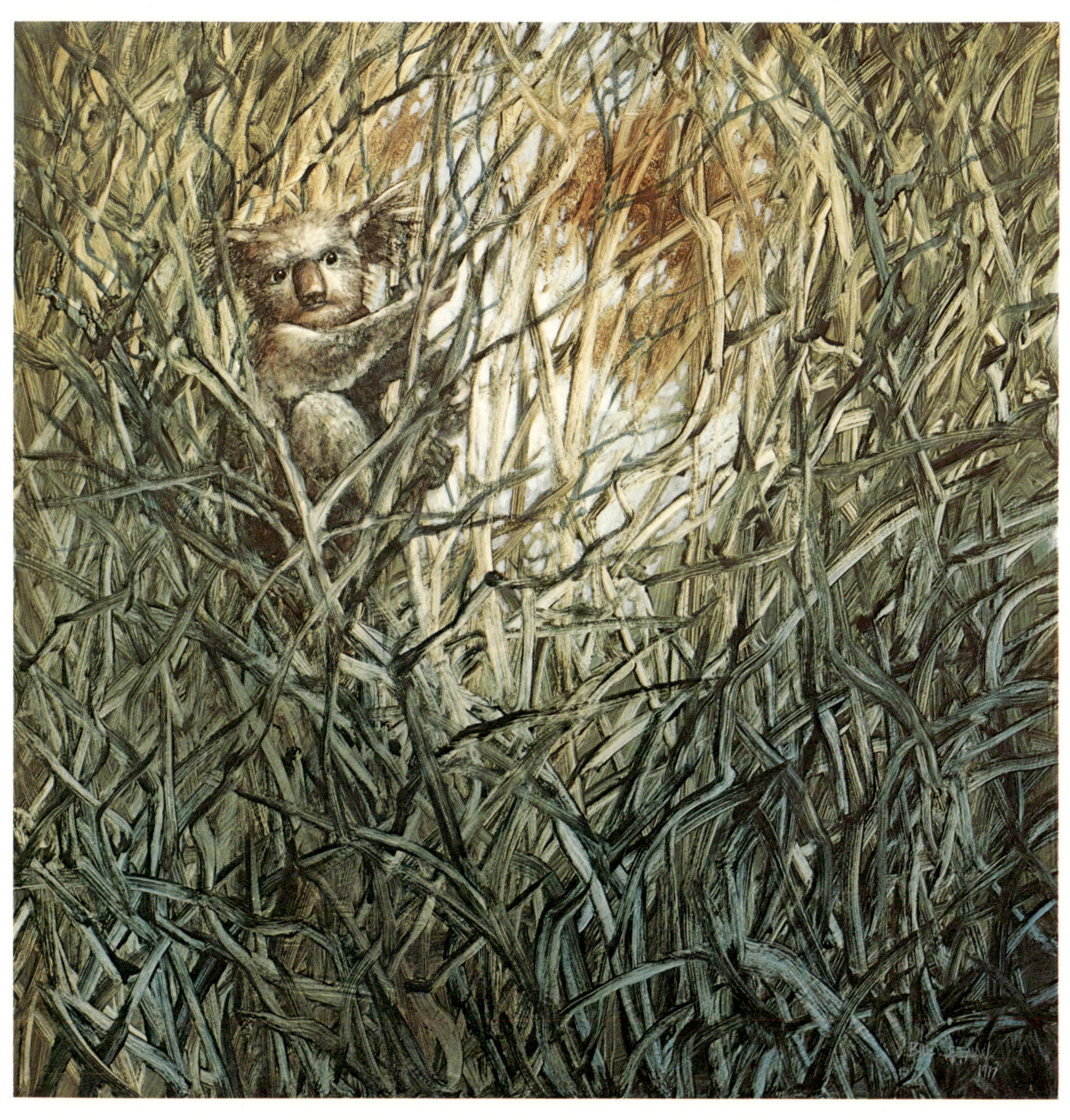

Green tangle of the brushes,
Where lithe lianas coil,

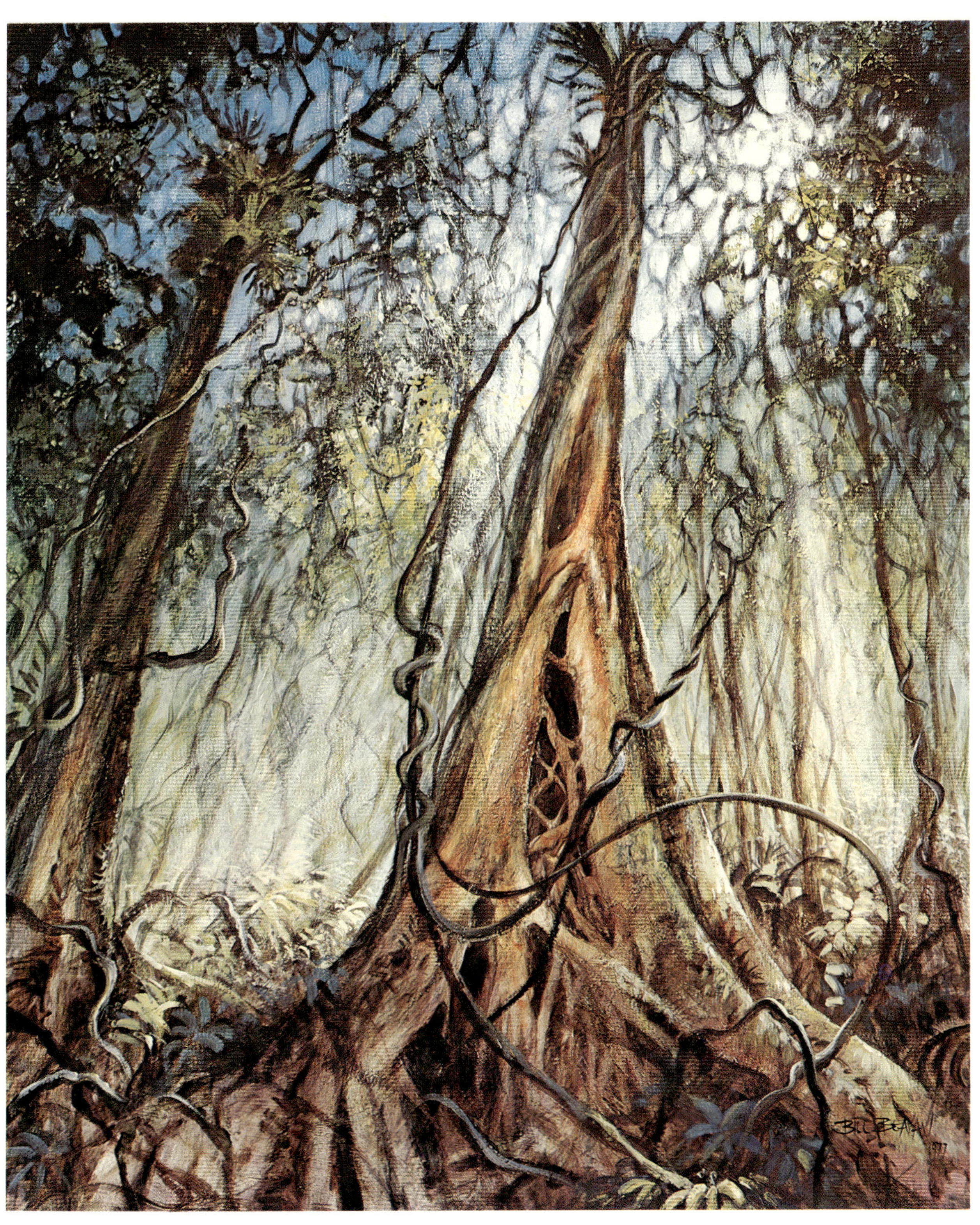

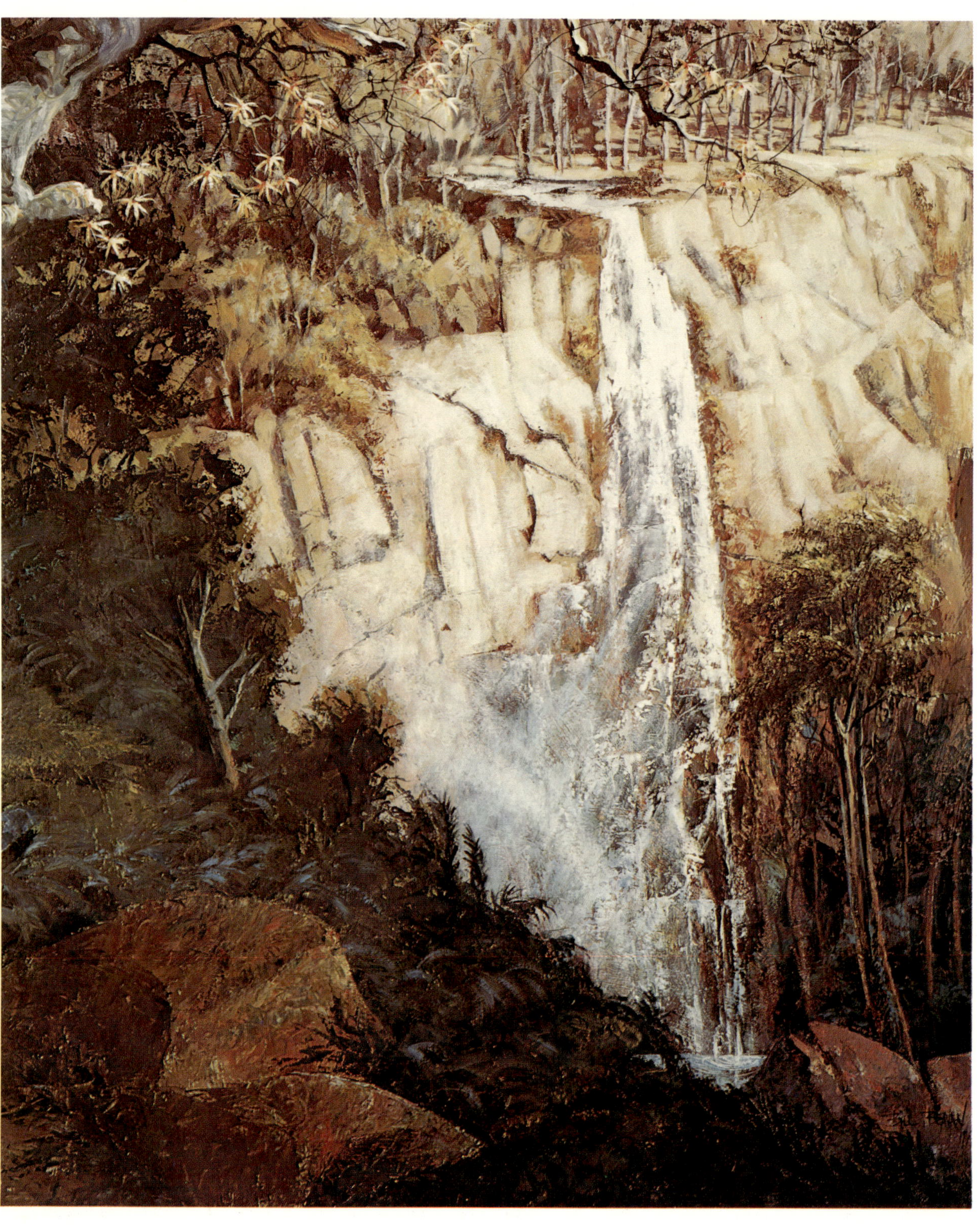

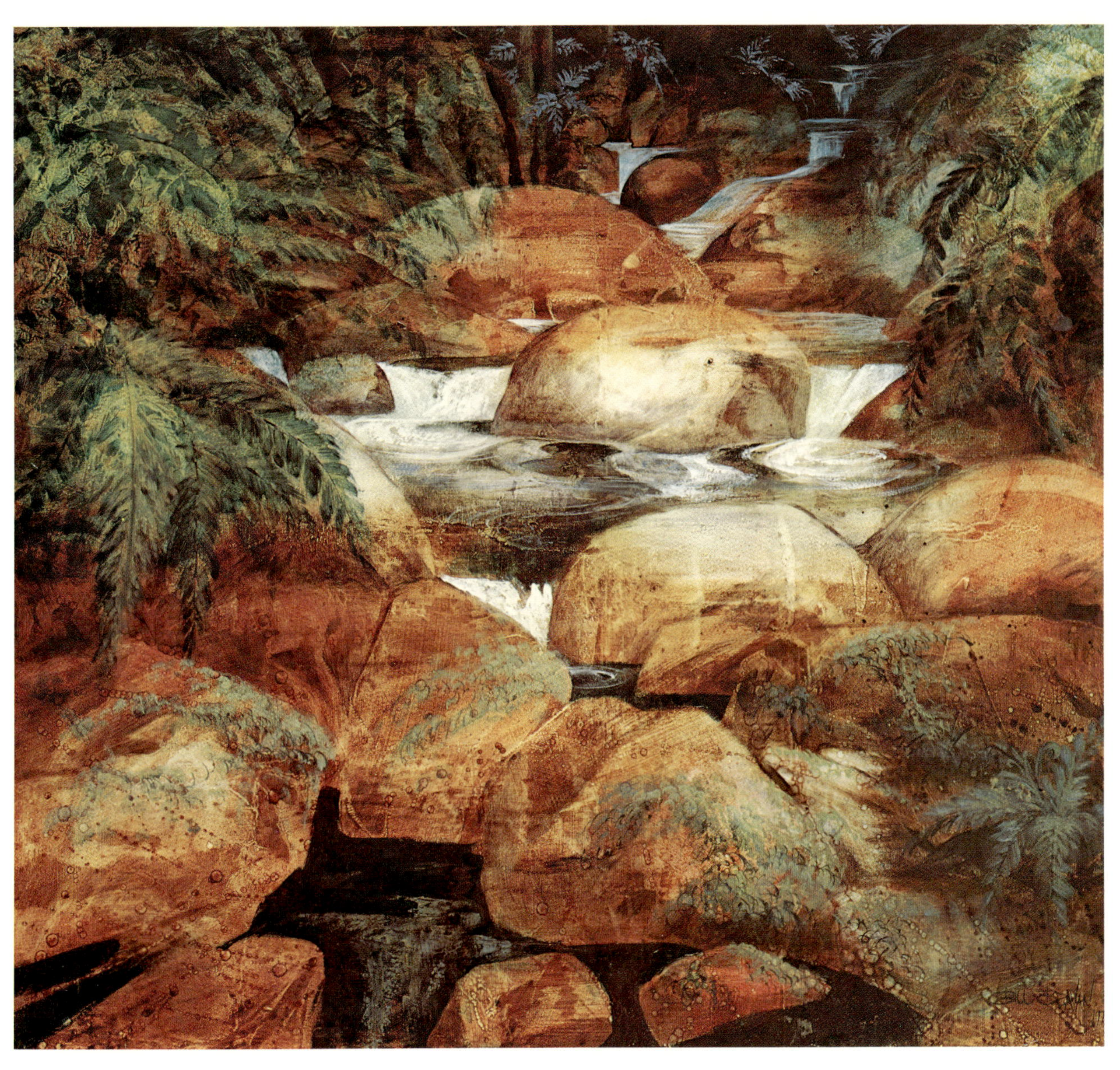

And orchids deck the tree-tops,
And ferns the warm dark soil.

Core of my heart my country,
Her pitiless blue sky,

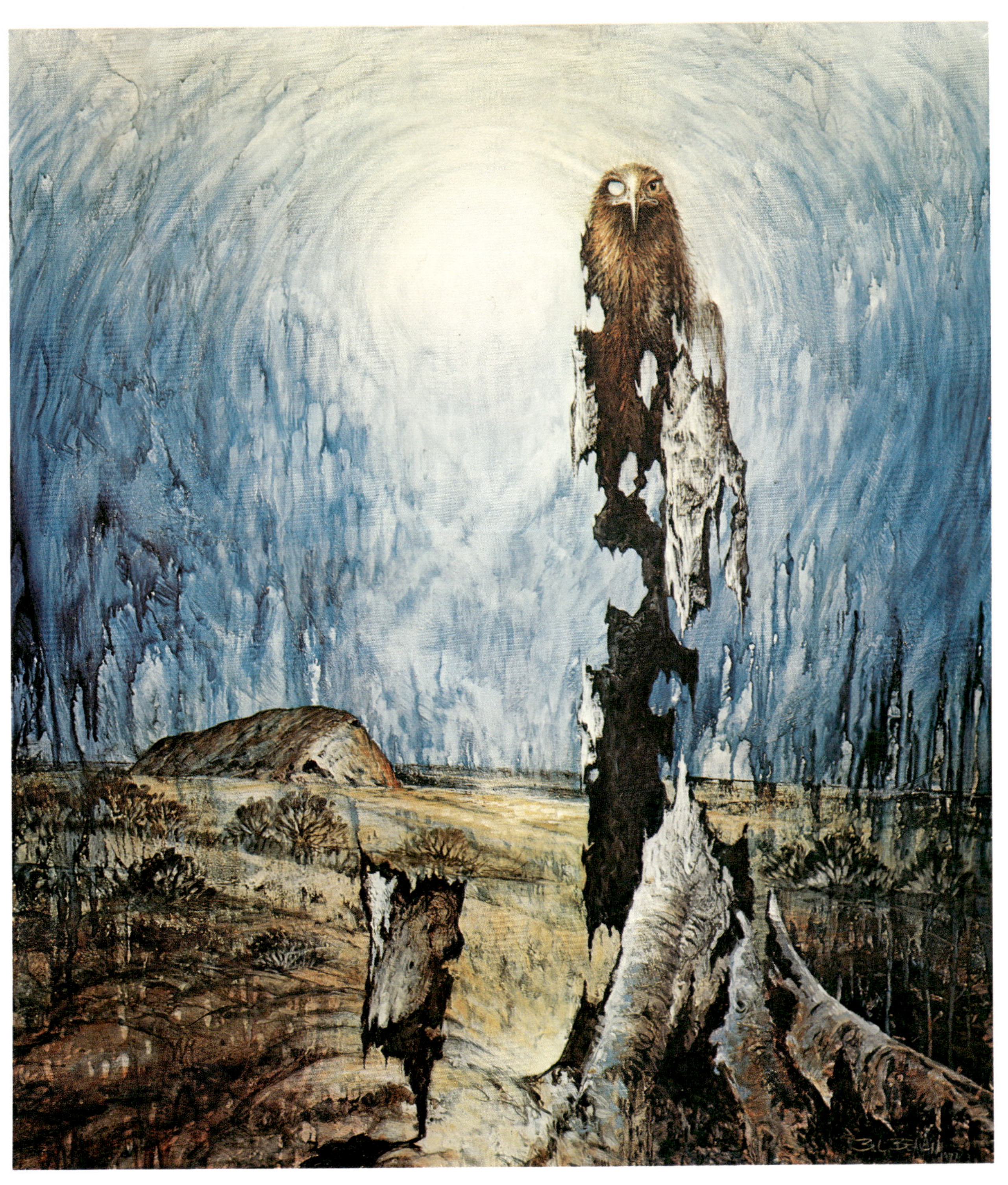

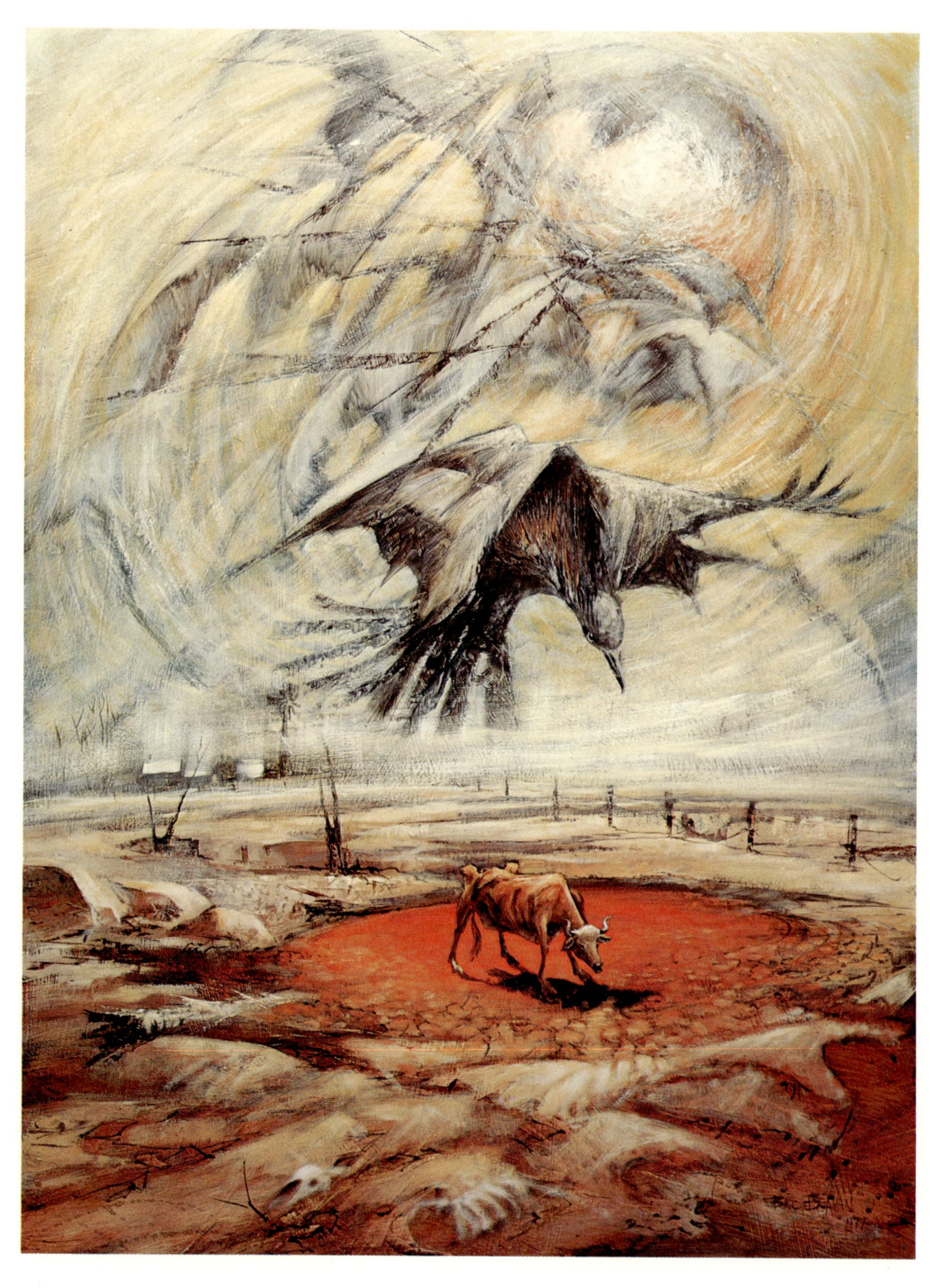

When sick at heart around us
We see the cattle die—

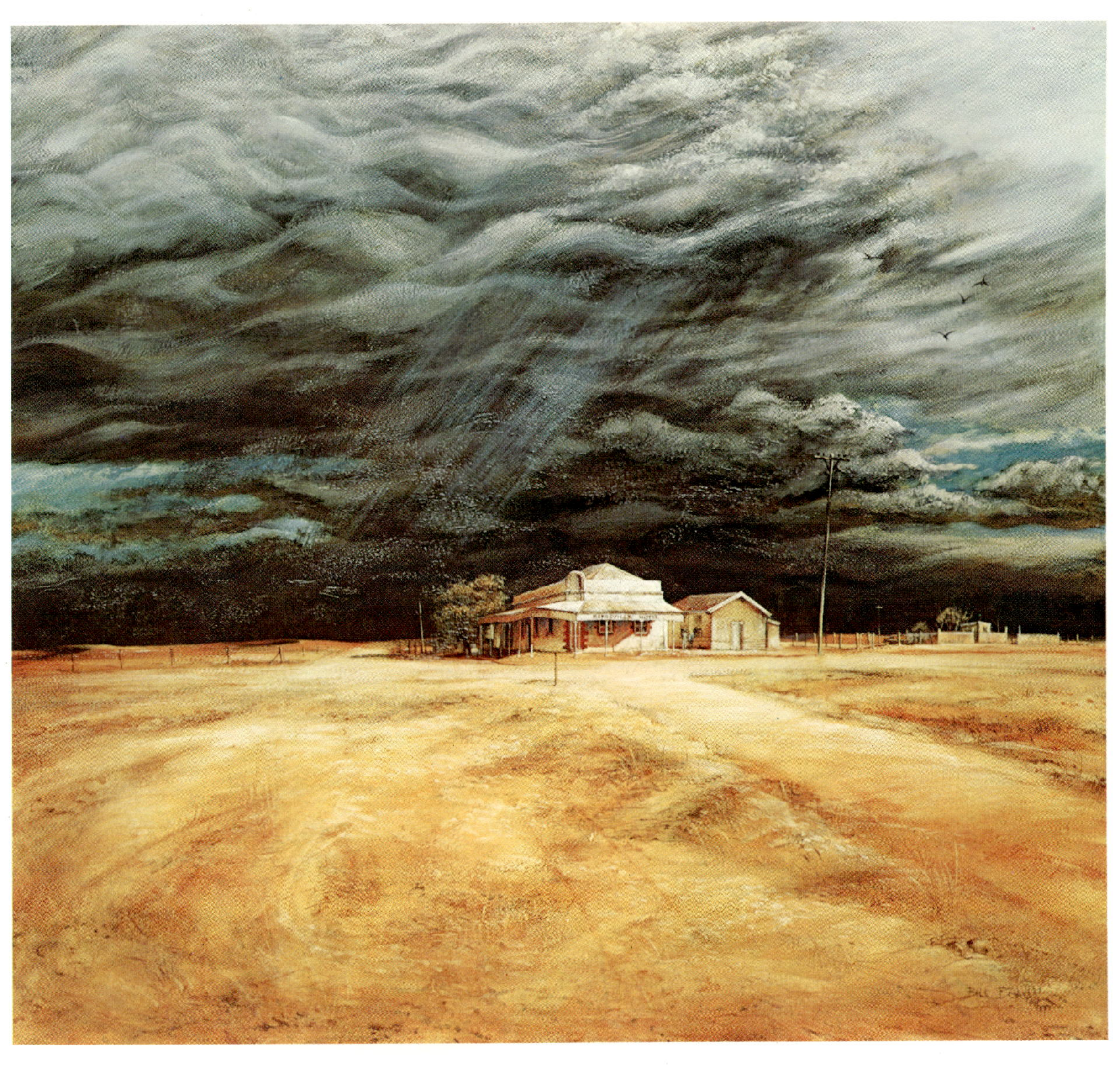

But then the grey clouds gather,
And we can bless again
The drumming of an army,

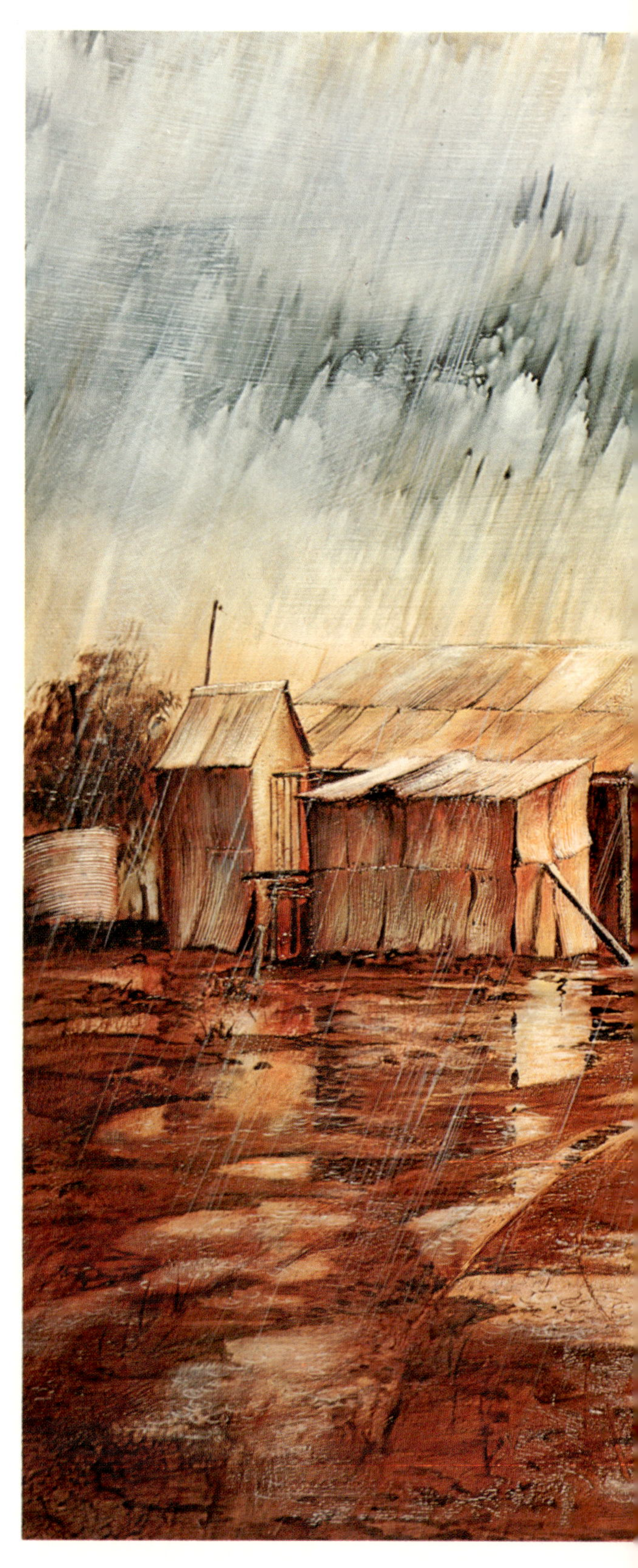

The steady soaking rain.

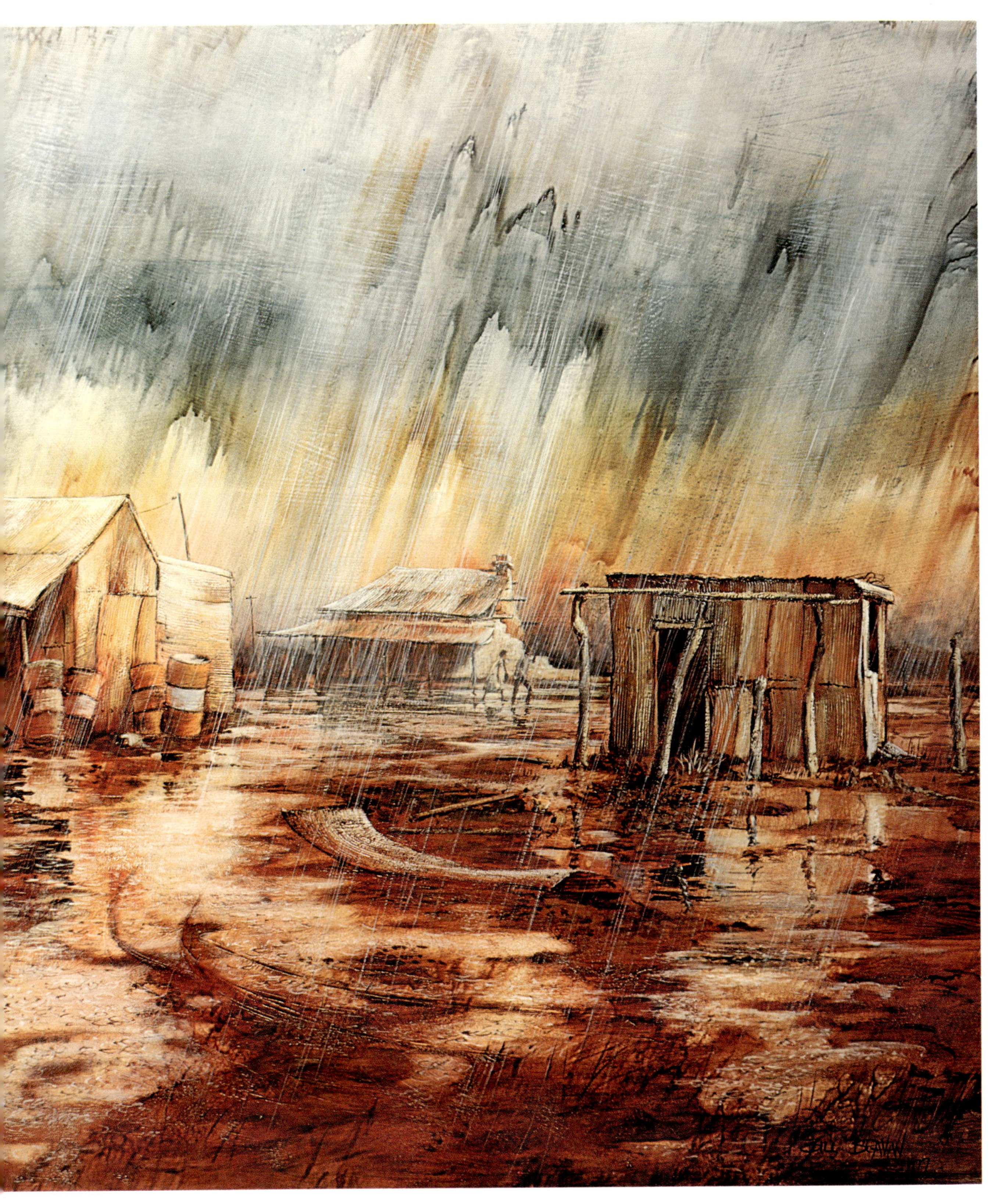

Core of my heart, my country!
Land of the Rainbow Gold,

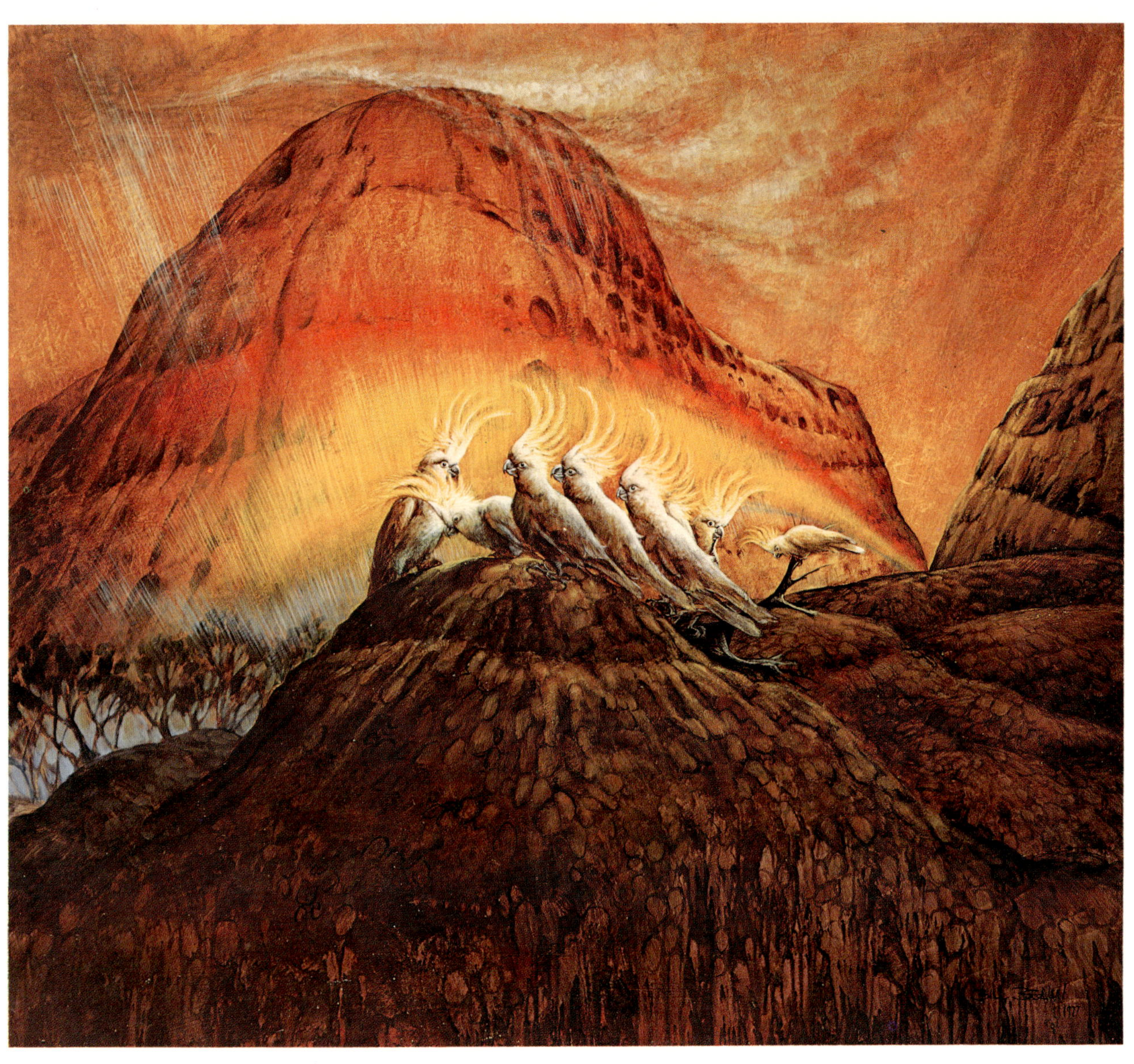

For flood and fire and famine,
She pays us back threefold;

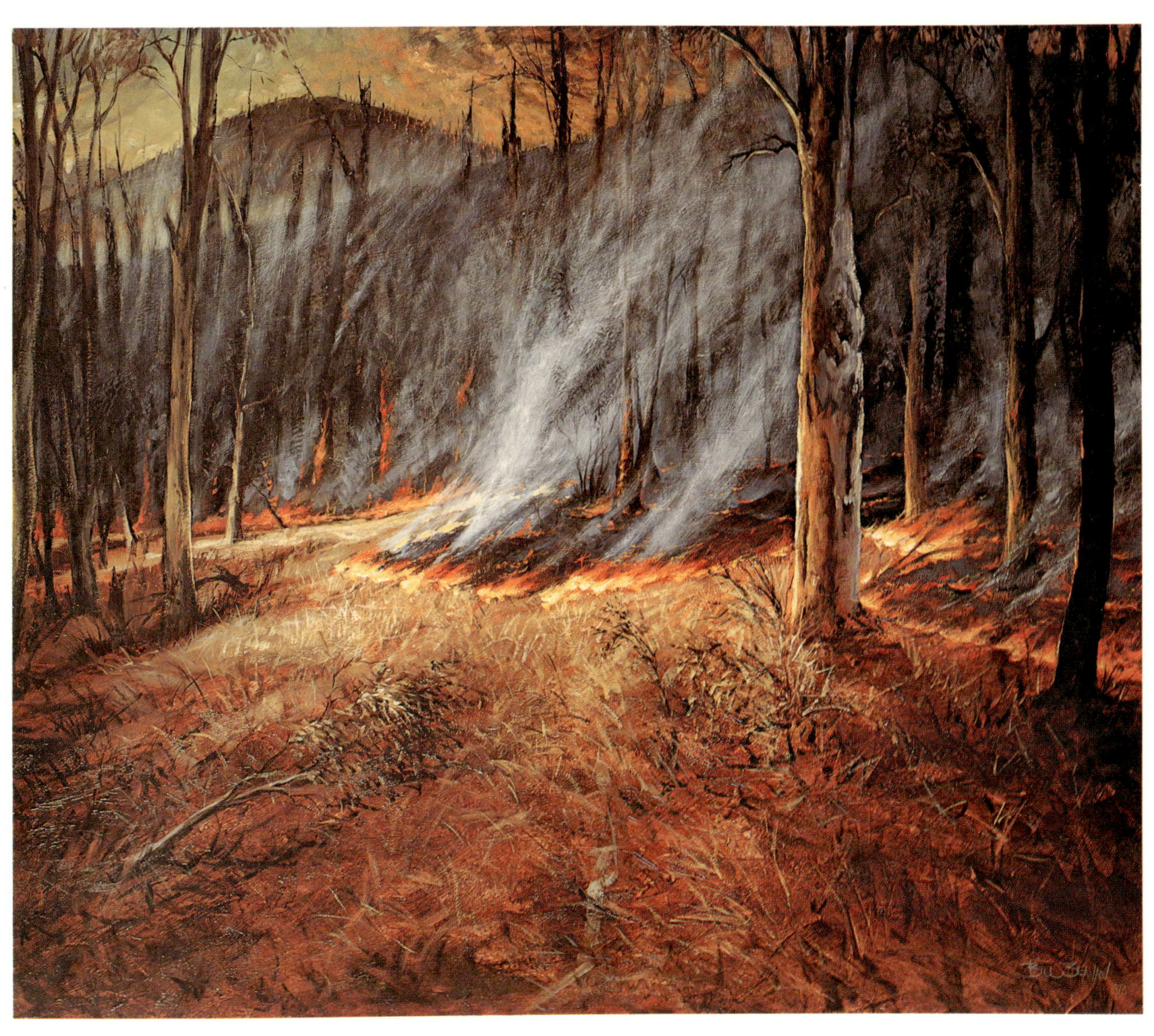

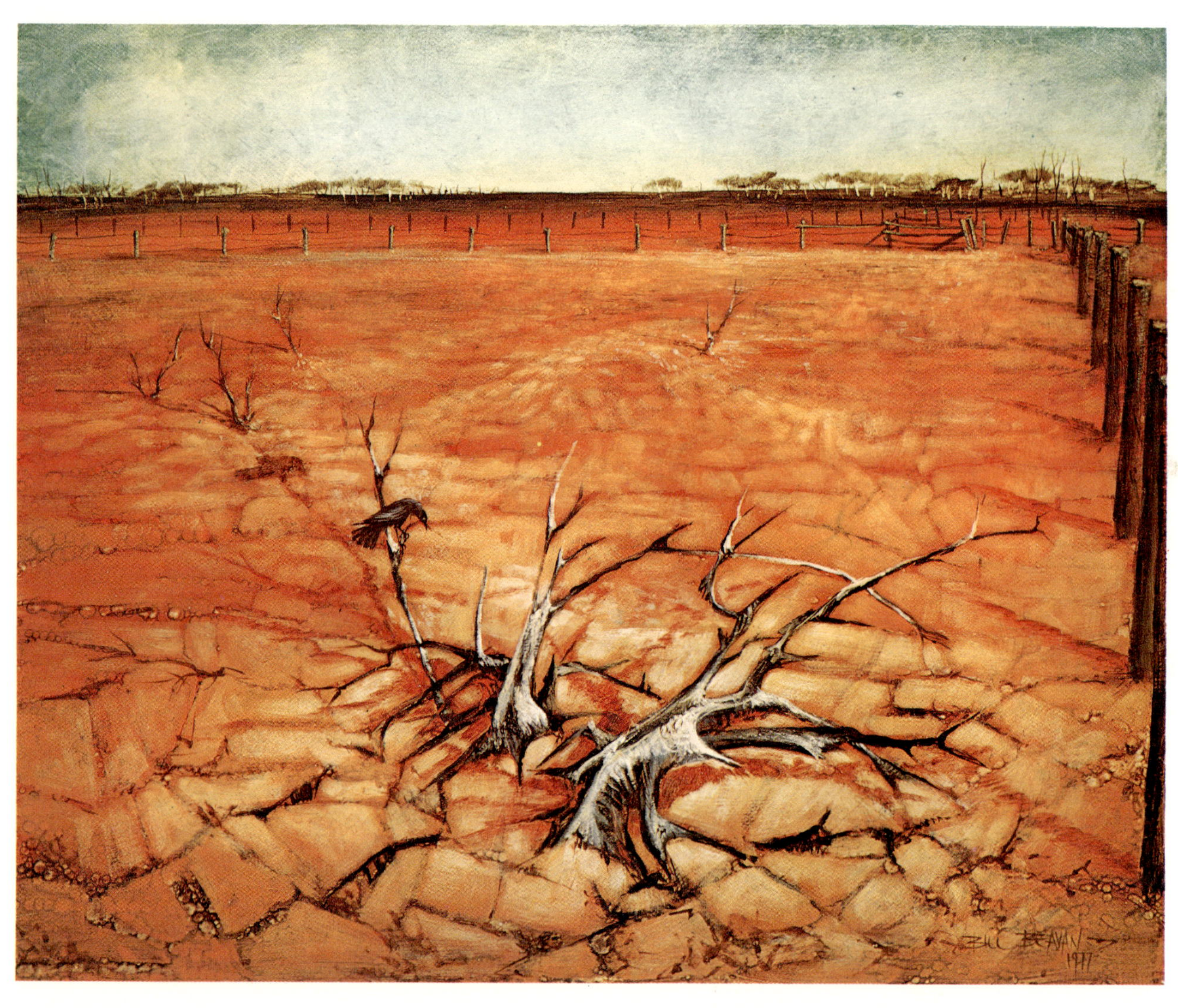

Over the thirsty paddocks,
Watch, after many days,

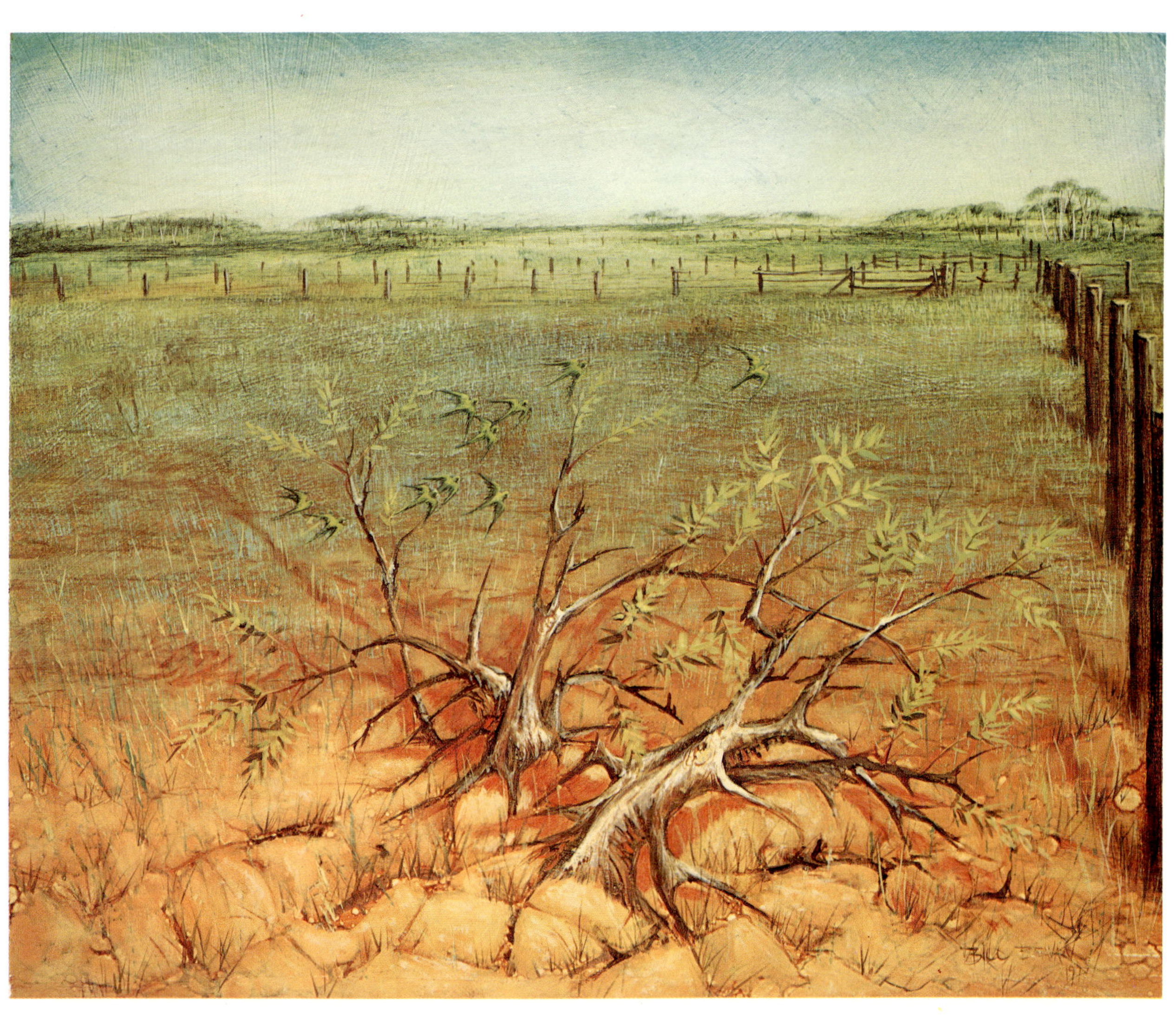

The filmy veil of greenness
That thickens as we gaze.

An opal-hearted country,

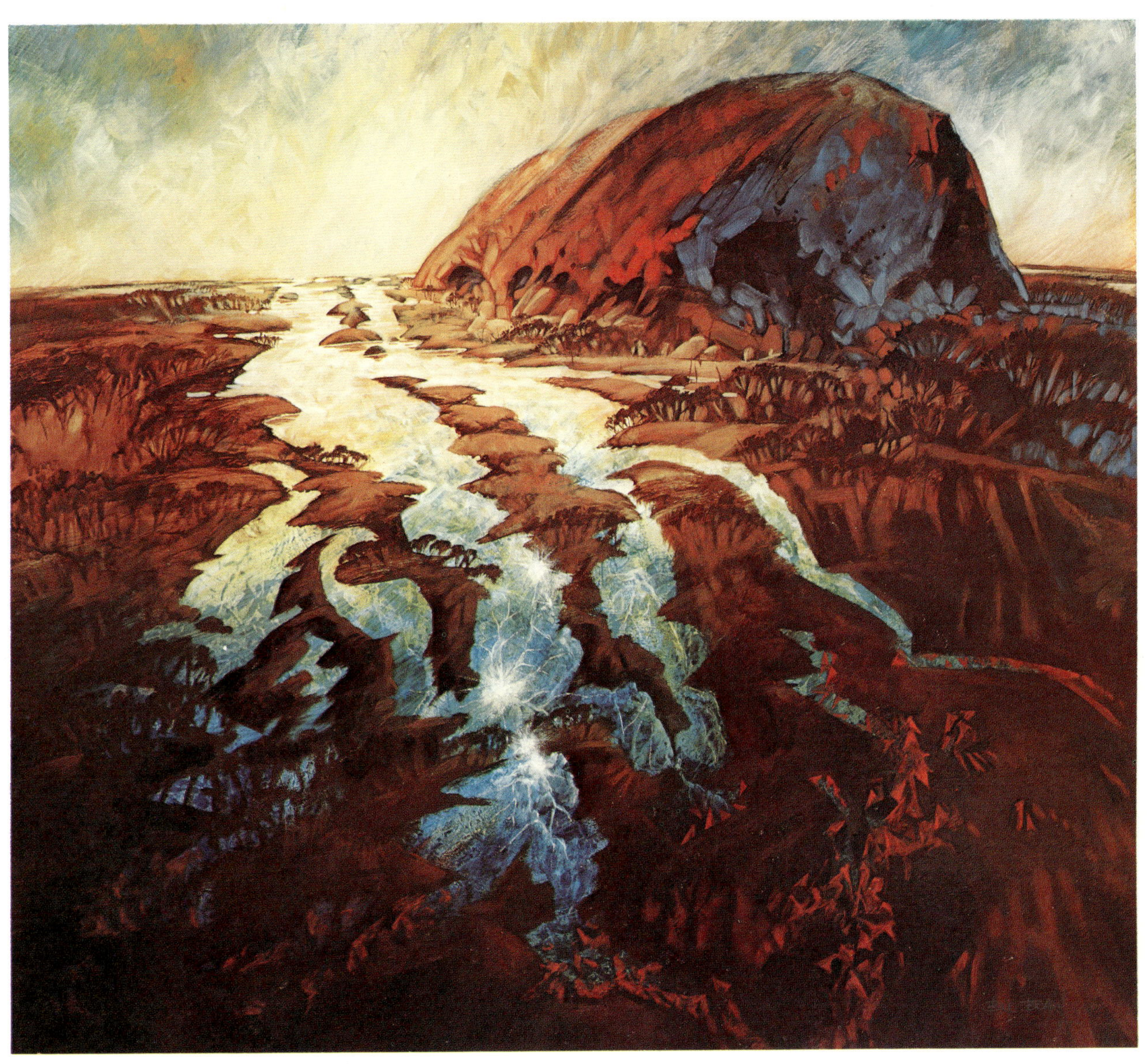

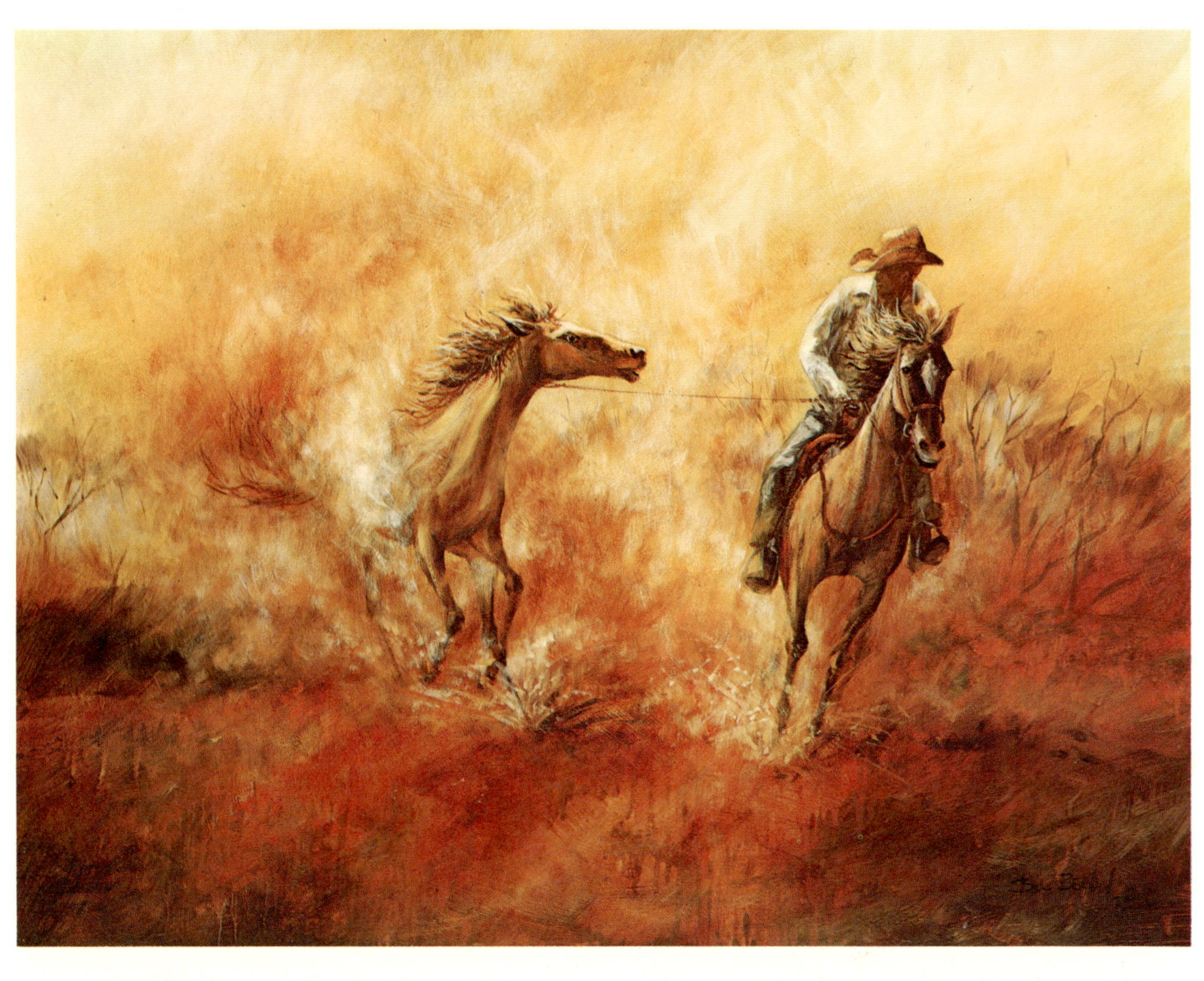

A wilful, lavish land—
All you who have not loved her,

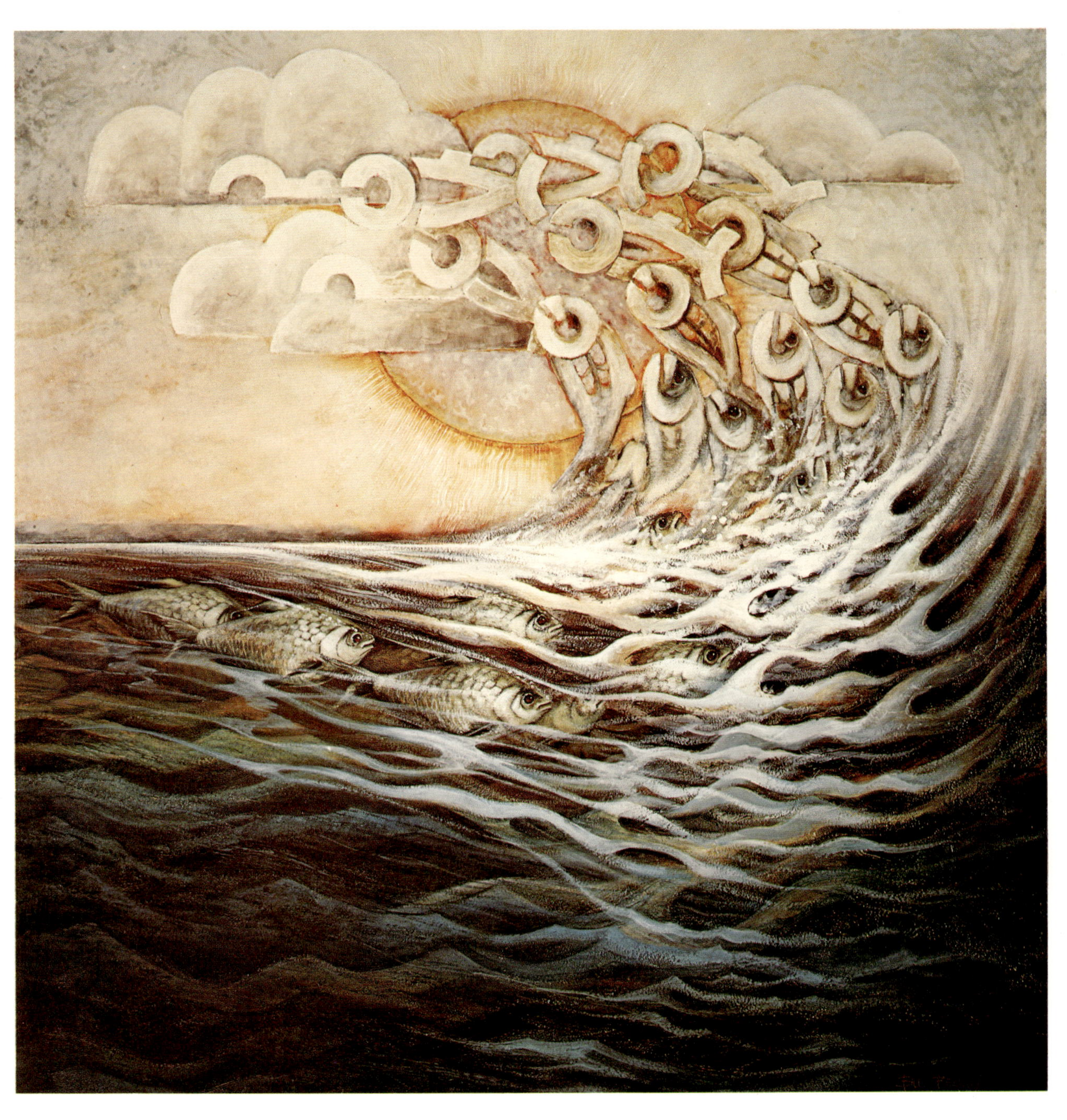

You will not understand—
Though earth holds many splendours,

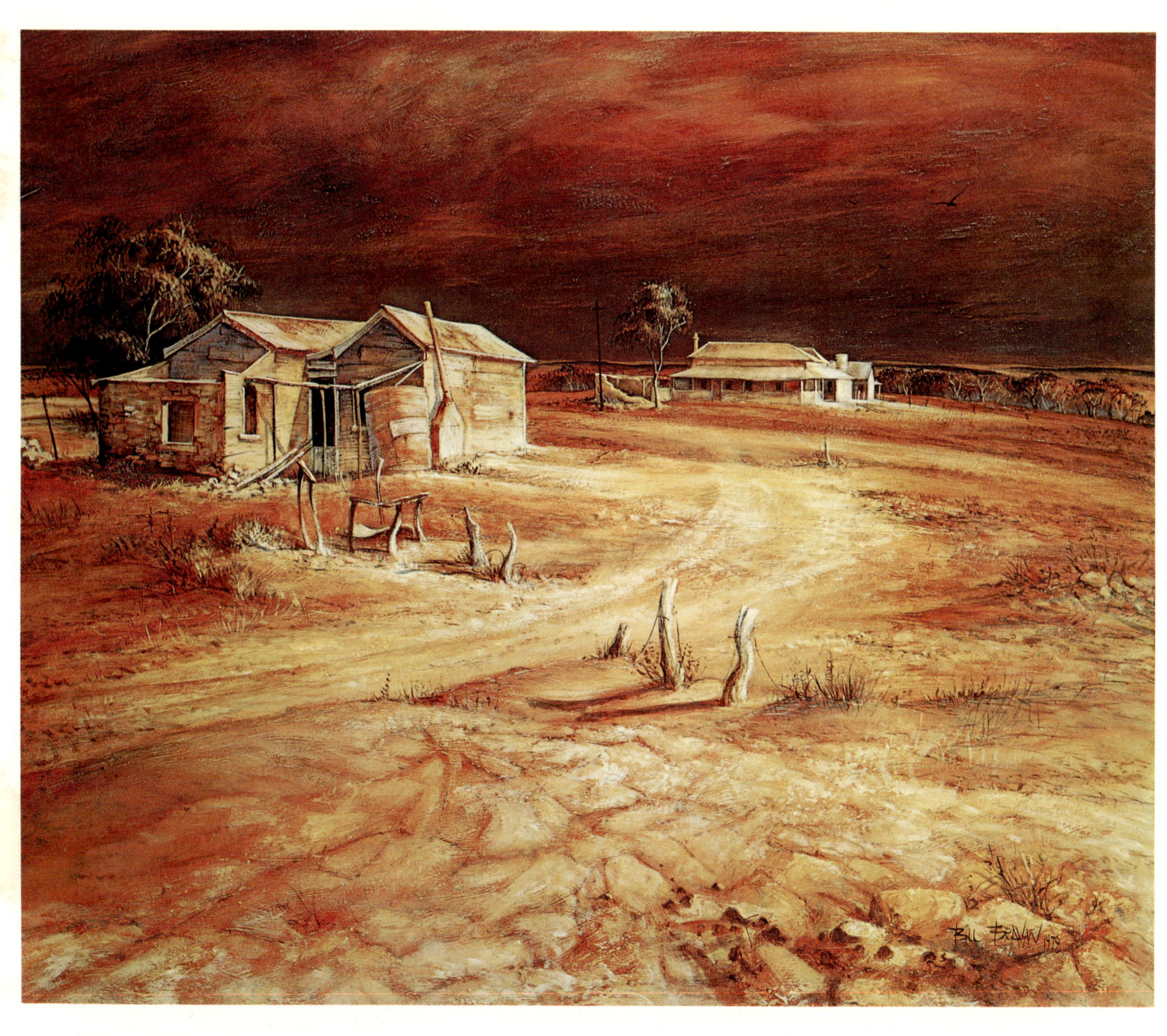

Wherever I may die,

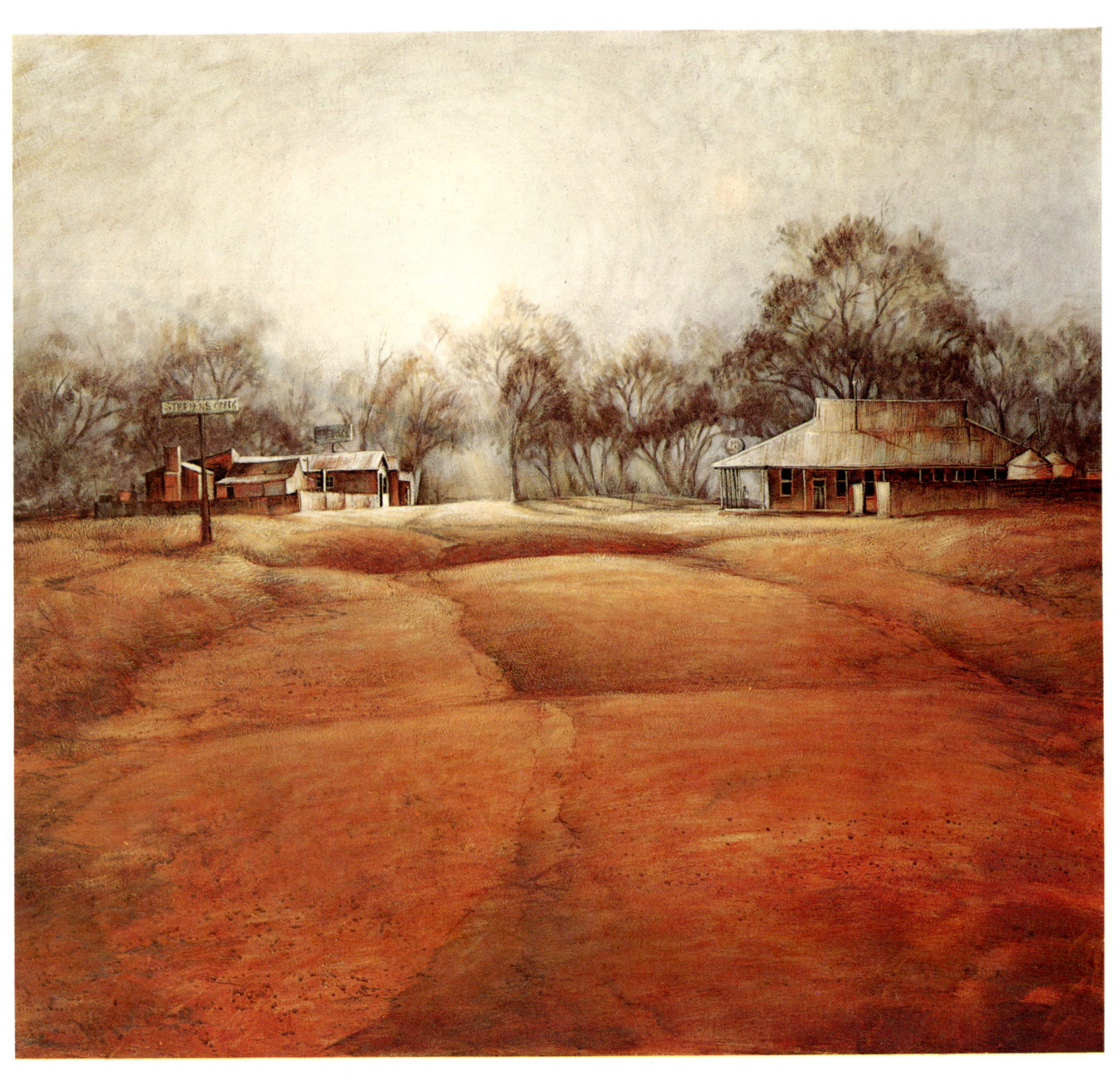

I know to what brown country
My homing thoughts will fly.

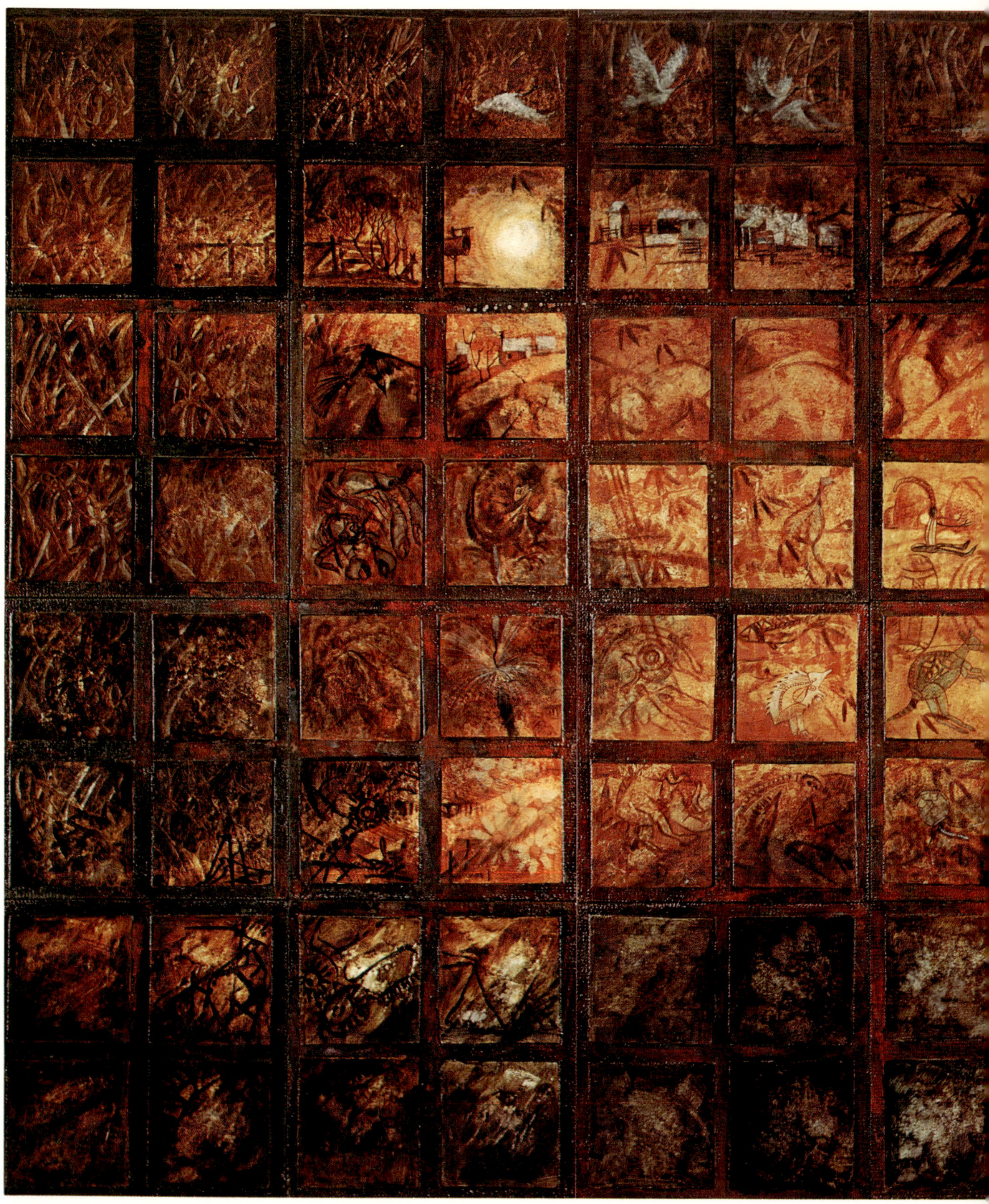

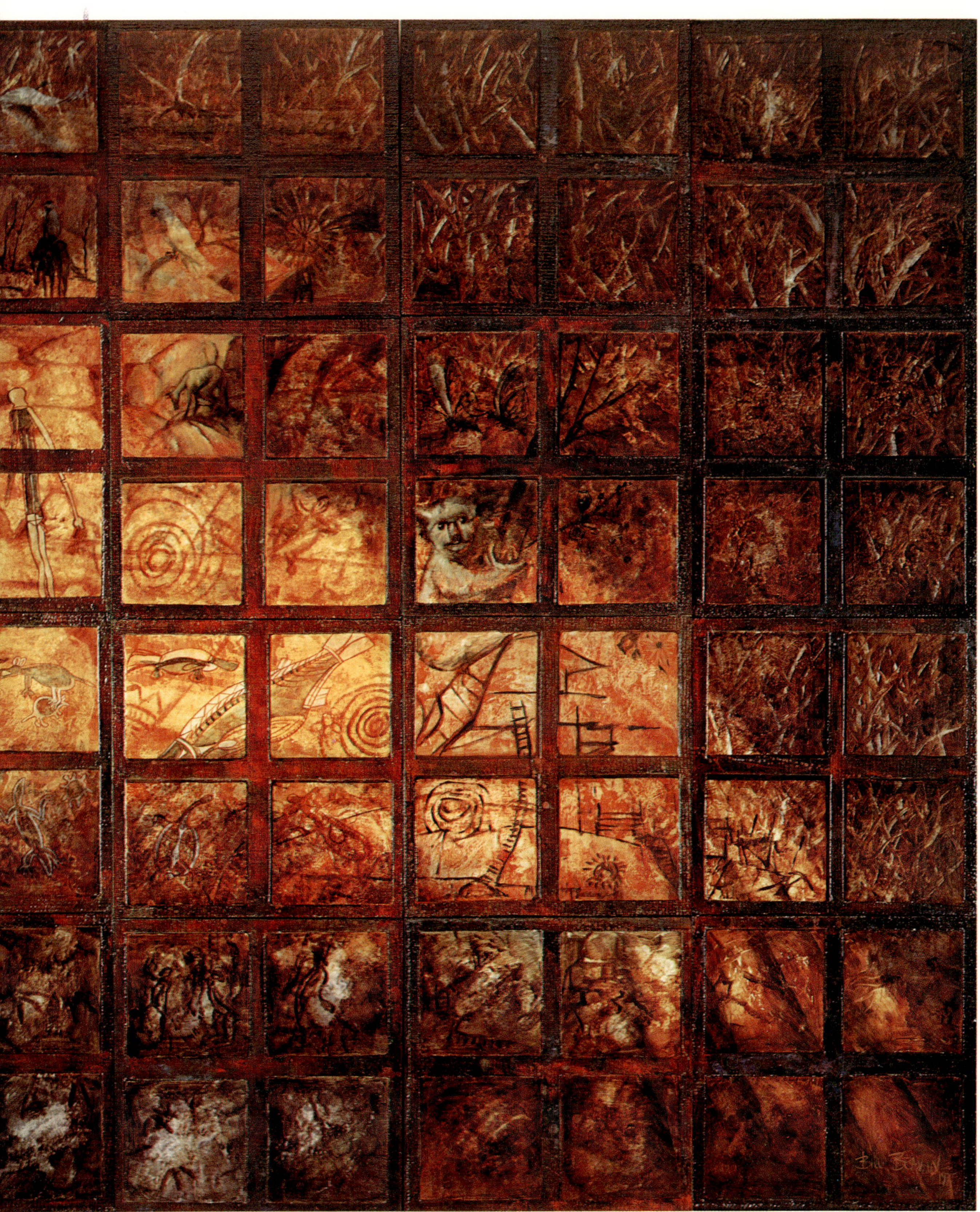

Notes on Plates

Page

17. *"Sunburnt Country"*, Hawker, S.A. Oil on Hardboard, 90cm × 80cm. Once a town thriving on the mining and farming industries, the old hotel crumbling away in the sun and wind, is typical of Hawker.

19. *"Sweeping Plains"*, Muloorina Station, S.A. Oil on Hardboard, 100cm × 90cm. After years of drought, the rains come and flowers cover the landscape like a carpet.

20. *"Ragged Mountain Ranges"*, Flinders Ranges, S.A. Oil on Hardboard, 100cm × 90cm. Thousands of years after the rock was thrust up from the flat plains, the peaks of the Flinders Ranges remain sharp and ragged.

21. *"Drought"*, Sturt's Stony Desert, S.A. Oil on Hardboard, 100cm × 90cm. The hot sun beats down on a frill-necked lizard.

22. *"Flooding Rains"*, The Coorong, S.A. Oil on Hardboard, 90cm × 80cm. Bird life feeds on the fish brought by winter floods to the salty marshes of the Coorong.

23. *"Far Horizons"*, The Channel Country, Qld. Oil on Hardboard, 120cm × 75cm. Tree-lined creek beds, waterless in drought, furrow the empty plains of the Channel Country.

25. *"The Jewel Sea"*, Flinders, Vic. Oil on Hardboard, 90cm × 80cm. The light of the setting sun catches drops of salt spray from waves as they pound the rocky shore.

26. *"Beauty"*, Cohuna, Vic. Oil on Hardboard, 70cm × 56cm. The white-feathered Egrets are famous for their graceful dance.

27. *"Terror"*, Arkaroola, S.A. Oil on Hardboard, 74cm × 86cm. Terrified by a sudden electric storm on a still day, all creatures run for cover.

29. *"The Wide Brown Land"*, White Cliffs, N.S.W. Oil on Hardboard, 100cm × 90cm. The dwellings of opal diggers break the outline of the endless brown plains.

31. *"Stark White Ring-Barked Forest"*, Ingebyra, N.S.W. Oil on Hardboad, 68cm × 90cm. Brolgas dance in the moonlight amongst the eerie ring-barked gums.

32. *"Sapphire Misted Mountains"*, Snowy Mountains N.S.W. Oil on Canvas, 90cm × 80cm. The blue mist reaches far into the distance of the Snowy Mountain Ranges.

33. *"Hot Gold Hush of Noon"*, Wilcannia, N.S.W. Oil on Hardboard, 100cm × 76cm. Man and horse shelter from blazing heat in the meagre shade of a gum tree.

34. *"Green Tangle"*, Townsville, Qld. Oil on Hardboard, 90cm × 90cm. Deep in the rain forests of the northern Great Dividing Ranges, the Koala peers out from tangled bush.

35. *"Where Lithe Lianas Coil"*, Lamington, Qld. Oil on Hardboard, 76cm × 90cm. Fighting their way up to the light, vines swirl around the trees in the rain forests.

36. *"Orchid Decked Tree-Tops"*, Lamington, Qld. Oil on Hardboard, 76cm × 90cm. As if suspended in the rising mist, the orchids bloom.

37. *"And Ferns the Warm Dark Soil"*, Lamington, Qld. Oil on Hardboard 90cm × 80cm. Under the canopy of leaves, ferns dip their fronds into the running water.

39. *"The Pitiless Blue Sky"*, Ayers Rock National Park, N.T. Oil on Hardboard, 90cm × 100cm. On the desolate gibber plains a brooding eagle stares down from its vantage point on a burnt-out tree stump.

40. *"The Cattle Die"*, Pooncarie, N.S.W. Oil on Hardboard, 68cm × 90cm. After the good years, drought strikes.

41. *"Grey Clouds Gather"*, Birdsville, Qld. Oil on Hardboard, 100cm × 90cm. The golden glow of the sun contrasts with approaching storm.

43. *"Steady Soaking Rain"*, Birdsville, Qld. Oil on Hardboard, 90cm × 70cm. Torrential rain turns the parched earth into quagmire.

45. *"Land of the Rainbow Gold"*, The Olgas, N.T. Oil on Hardboard, 90cm × 80cm. A rainbow silhouettes sulphur-crested cockatoos, poised like dancers on a stage.

47. *"Land of Fire"*, Noojee, Vic. Oil on Hardboard, 90cm × 76cm. Bushfire leaves a blackened landscape to complete another cycle of life in the forest.

48. *"Thirsty Paddocks"*, Balranald, N.S.W. Oil on Hardboard, 60cm × 50cm. Dry earth cracks during the long drought.

49. *"A Filmy Veil of Greenness"*, Balranald, N.S.W. Oil on Hardboard, 60cm × 50cm. And when the drought breaks, green grass brings renewed life.

51. *"An Opal-Hearted Country"*, Ayers Rock, N.T. Oil on Hardboard, 90cm × 80cm. Pools of water mirror the illusive colours of Ayers Rock at Sunset.

52. *"A Wilful Land"*, Menindee, N.S.W. Oil on Hardboard, 70cm × 56cm. The wild brumby symbolizes the spirit of the outback.

53. *"You Will Not Understand"*, Lake Eyre, S.A. Enamel on Canvas, 168cm × 168cm. In Aboriginal legend, to explain what they could not understand, the fish become clouds and return again with the rain.

54.
Cover "Farina", Farina, S.A. Oil on Hardboard, 60cm × 50cm. Now a dusty ghost-town, Farina was once the staging depot for the camel trains which travelled the Strzelecki track to Innamincka and beyond.

55. *"A Brown Country"*, Stephens Creek, N.S.W. Oil on Hardboard, 100cm × 90cm. The monotony of brown country is broken by trees growing along a creek bed.

56/57 *"Thoughts Will Fly"*. Enamel on Hessian, 320cm × 184cm. Memories of outback Australia form a mosaic of glowing colour and timeless images.

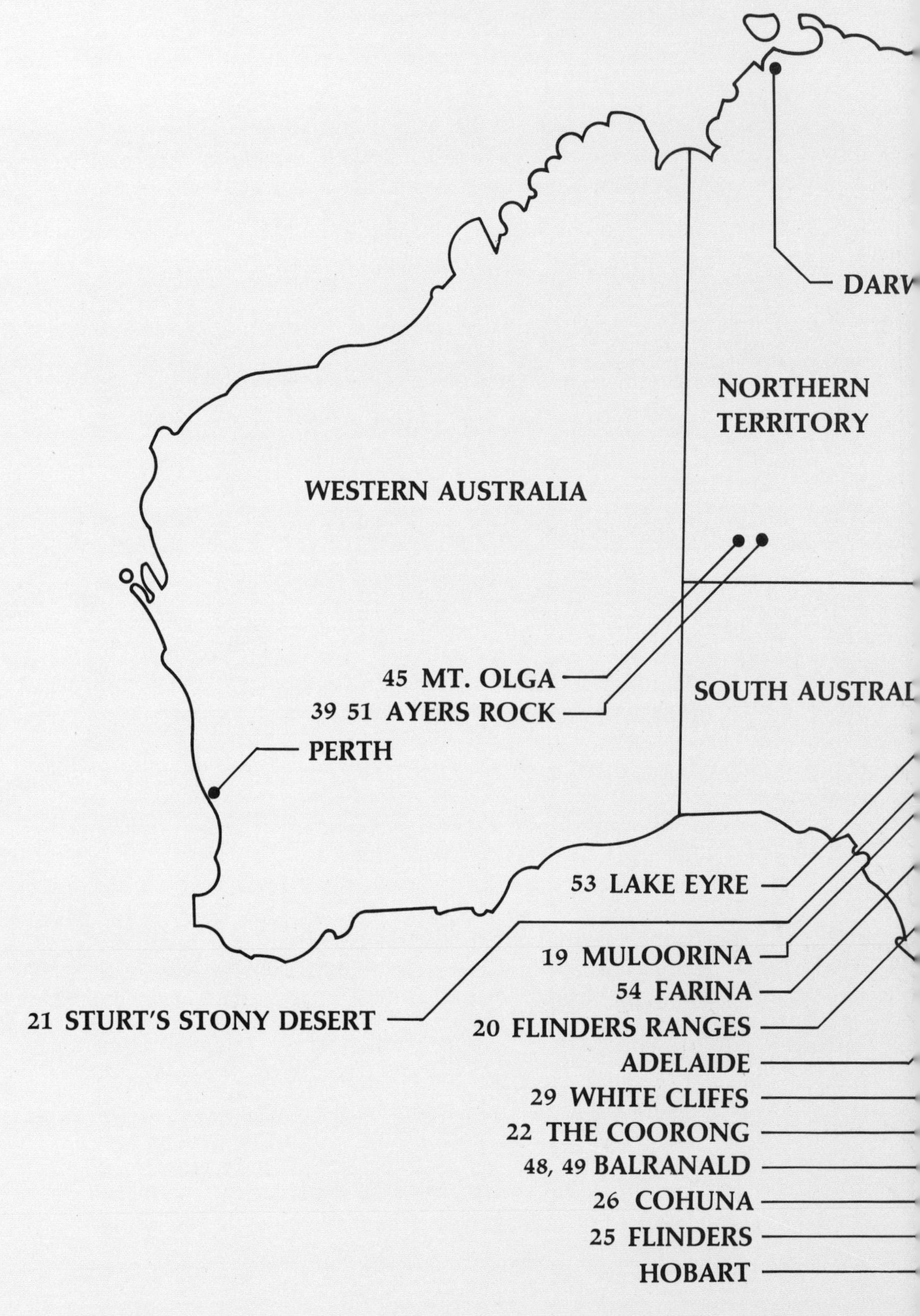
DARV
NORTHERN TERRITORY
WESTERN AUSTRALIA
45 MT. OLGA
39 51 AYERS ROCK
SOUTH AUSTRAL
PERTH
53 LAKE EYRE
19 MULOORINA
54 FARINA
21 STURT'S STONY DESERT
20 FLINDERS RANGES
ADELAIDE
29 WHITE CLIFFS
22 THE COORONG
48, 49 BALRANALD
26 COHUNA
25 FLINDERS
HOBART

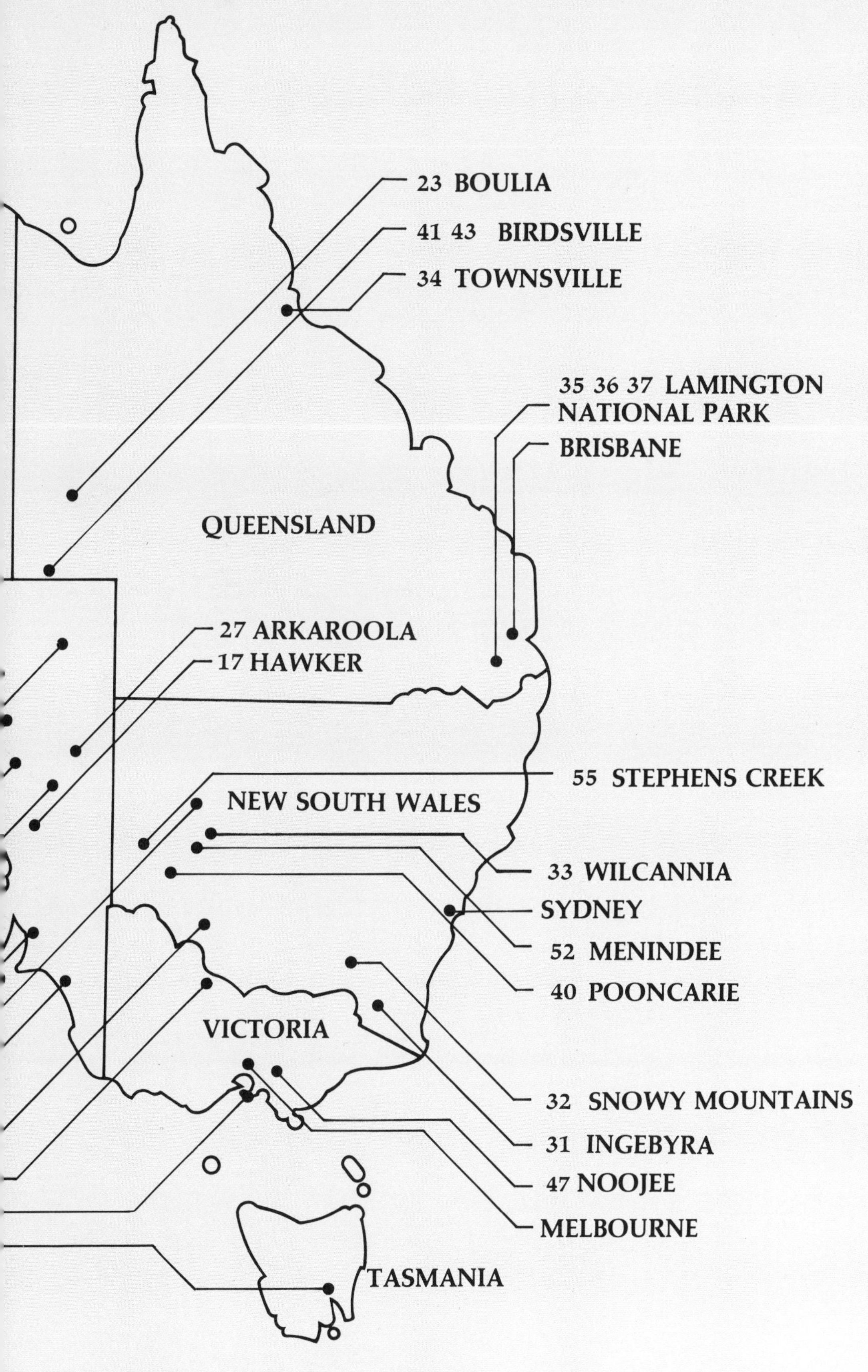

23 BOULIA
41 43 BIRDSVILLE
34 TOWNSVILLE
35 36 37 LAMINGTON NATIONAL PARK
BRISBANE
QUEENSLAND
27 ARKAROOLA
17 HAWKER
55 STEPHENS CREEK
NEW SOUTH WALES
33 WILCANNIA
SYDNEY
52 MENINDEE
40 POONCARIE
VICTORIA
32 SNOWY MOUNTAINS
31 INGEBYRA
47 NOOJEE
MELBOURNE
TASMANIA